COMMUNITY INITIATIVES

COMMUNITY INITIATIVES

PATTERNS AND PROSPECTS

PETER WILLMOTT

Policy Studies Institute

PSI Publications are obtainable from all good bookshops, or by visiting the Institute at 100 Park Village East, London NW1 3SR (01-387 2171).

Sales Representation: Pinter Publishers Ltd.

Individual and Bookshop orders to: Marston Book Services Ltd, PO Box 87, Oxford, OX4 1LB.

A CIP catalogue record of this book is available from the British Library

PSI Research Report 698

ISBN 0 85374 346 0

Laserset by Policy Studies Institute

Printed by Blackmore Press, Longmead, Shaftesbury, Dorset

Contents

Preface and Acknowledgements

This report is in two parts. The first is a broad review of the introduction of the notion of community into public policy and social life in recent decades. The aims of the review are to analyse the different ways in which community labels have been applied and to assess their contribution.

The second part is a series of case studies examining different applications. These studies provide the material on which the broader discussion is based. The case studies will be of particular interest to people in the different fields, but they are non-technical enough to make sense to non-specialists as well.

The research was funded by the Joseph Rowntree Memorial Trust. Valuable help was given by David Thomas in the initial phase of the research. The following commented on draft reports or helped in other ways: Gabriel Chanin, David Donnison, Colin Fletcher, David Jones, Rupert Nabarro, John Nisbet, Marylin Taylor, Gerry Williams, Phyllis Willmott and Charles Woodd, together with PSI colleagues Isobel Allen, Naomi Connelly and Eileen Reid. The study was assisted by an advisory group, whose membership changed after the initial phase. The members were: Martin Bulmer, Paul Curno, Nicholas Deakin, Hywell Griffiths, Barry Knight, Jim Jackson, Paul McQuail, Richard Mills, Roy Parker, Judy Weleminsky and Peter Westland. Robin Guthrie, then Director of the Joseph Rowntree Memorial Trust, chaired the advisory group and was helpful throughout.

PART I   DISCUSSION

1 Introduction

When the history of British social policy in the latter half of the 20th century comes to be written, the concept of community and its influence on public policy and public endeavour will certainly figure. What we cannot know is how it will be judged, how far it will be seen as marking a genuine change in ways of organising our collective life, how far a rhetorical exploitation of high-minded ambiguity.

Community ideas have gained momentum over about a quarter of a century. They took hold slowly at first. Community education had started to develop before the Second World War, and ideas of community centres and associations had stirred while that war was on, to be quietly forgotten after 1945. Town planners continued to take some interest in neighbourhoods (mainly in the new towns), but the concept of community hardly figured in public discourse until the late 1950s.

In 1957 the Royal Commission on the Law Relating to Mental Illness and Mental Deficiency was in advance of its time in explicitly advocating a policy to which the concept of community was integral. 'There should', said the Commission, 'be a general re-orientation away from institutional care in its present form and towards community care'[1]. The example gradually spread within the health and welfare services, and the terminology and the idea were taken up in more and more other fields. Now the word is everywhere, from community bookshops to community planning, from community broadcasting to community enterprise, from community transport to community dance. As well as the cases examined in Part II, the Appendix, which includes brief notes on further examples, gives some indication of the range of applications.

The continuing popularity of the concept is illustrated by three recent examples. In 1986 the government announced its proposals for a community charge, in 1987 local chemists started to describe themselves as community pharmacists, and in the same year the Post Office decided to reclassify most of its 8,000 rural sub offices as community post offices.

Word and meaning
The popularity of the word has not made its meaning any clearer. If anything, it is used even more ambiguously than in the past. At times the multiplicity and variety of applications seem so diverse as to render the term almost meaningless.

The essence of the word, as all etymological explanations show, is the idea of 'having something in common'. Among all the confusion, however, there is widespread agreement about one important semantic distinction: it is recognised that community can refer to the population of a particular geographical area – the 'territorial community' – or to people who share in common something other than physical proximity in the same place.

The territorial community in question can vary widely in scale; it can be as small as a few streets or as large as a nation (or even a group of them, as in the European Community). In terms of both official policy and indigenous initiatives, the commonest scale is relatively small and local, and in this report attention is mainly focussed upon local communities – some of them small enough to be places to which the term neighbourhood could also be applied – but with some reference to larger territorial communities such as districts or boroughs, towns or cities.

For the second usage the term 'interest community' – or community of interest – has been adopted throughout the English-speaking world. An alternative term – 'interest group' – is sometimes used. It is recognised that what is shared in such a grouping of people is more than 'interest', as that word is normally understood; it can also cover characteristics as varied as ethnic origin, religion, politics, occupation, leisure pursuit and sexual propensity; it is applied for instance to the black community, the Jewish community, the lesbian community.

In recent years a new kind of interest community has developed in Britain, one that has important implications for social policy. This is the self-help or mutual aid group, composed of people who share a common condition or problem – examples are alcohol dependency, cancer, epilepsy, eczema and widowhood, and having stillborn children or children with a particular disability. A particular kind of self-help group is a credit union; it offers loans to its members from a pool of savings provided by the members themselves. Credit unions are in Britain registered under the Credit Union Act 1979, and they have to demonstrate that the members share a 'common bond', for example, being members of the same church, working for the same employer or (the territorial basis) living in the same geographical area[2].

The two concepts – the territorial community and the interest community – are not mutually exclusive. They can overlap in the sense that, although interest communities are often geographically dispersed, they can also exist inside even quite small areas. A local territorial community might contain several communities, such as communities of church and chapel goers, a community of business people and a community of Asian residents. Some self-help groups may be local in the sense that a group of widows, for example, who are living in the same neighbourhood may come together for mutual support. But most such groups operate on a wider geographical scale; they have to, because the particular minority is so small in proportionate terms that it needs to draw on a relatively large catchment population.

There is thus a second distinction, an important one which cuts across the first, between local and non-local communities. Local communities are territorial, but contain localised interest communities. Non-local communities – that is, communities at a larger territorial scale – also contain interest communities, which are geographically dispersed. I take up in the next chapter the question of how 'local' should be defined; all I need to say here is that there is a hierarchy of local communities from the immediate area – say a street or a block of flats – to a district or a town.

These two dimensions – territorial/interest and local/non-local – refer merely to collections of people. A local territorial community is simply the population of a particular local area. A dispersed interest community is a collection of people who have something in common, but do not live in the same geographical area.

But in common usage community does not necessarily refer just to the fact of people living in the same place or sharing the same interests or characteristics. People sometimes, but not always, recognise the common interests they share with others living in the same area or having the same characteristics. Sometimes, but not always, they have a feeling of identity, of common membership. So 'community' is sometimes used to refer to such sentiments or feelings, and to social bonds and patterns of behaviour that can sustain and reflect those sentiments and feelings. Terms like 'sense of community' and 'spirit of community' suggest the general sense of this third meaning of the word.

It is not easy to select an appropriate label for it, to be used alongside those already introduced. I call it the 'community of attachment' or 'attachment community'. A particular advantage of 'attachment' as a term is that it brings together the two key elements contained in this concept. One has to do with the extent and density of social relationships, the second with perceptions, with the extent to which people feel a sense of identity with a place or a group and of solidarity with their fellows living in it or sharing its interests or characteristics. It is legitimate to combine the two aspects into one notion because, as research has shown, at least at the local level they usually go together. They do so because they reinforce each other[3].

A key question is whether – or, to be more precise, to what extent – a particular territorial community or interest community is an attachment community as well. Particular places (to take the territorial example) are attachment communities to a greater or lesser degree, and the question is how much and how persistently. In practice, the proportion of people for whom it is an attachment community, and for how long, virtually determine how much and for how long the grouping as a whole is an attachment community.

Distinguishing these meanings of community – territorial, interest, local, non-local and degree of attachment – may have the advantage of drawing attention to the fact that, for example, the people living in a particular area do not always feel a sense of attachment to each other or to the place, nor necessarily share the same priorities as their neighbours; indeed in complex modern societies they seldom do either to any substantial extent. The distinction may also put us on our guard against the almost mystical feelings that can be stirred by the word community.

This 'warmly persuasive word', as Raymond Williams described it, can be applied either to 'an existing set of relationships' or an alternative set which may be realised in the future; in any event, as he said, 'it seems never to be used unfavourably'[4]. This is one of the reasons why it causes problems: the word hints at comforting nostalgia or exhortatory inspiration, at ideology or utopia. Because of these overtones, it can only too readily be employed in an emotionally-charged fashion, and it is not always clear whether the extra meaning – the benign sense of attachment – is being invoked or, if it is, how legitimately.

This is one of the dangers of using the term as a label. As David J. Smith has pointed out, it 'encourages skilful jumps' from one meaning to another[5]. It can conceal more than it reveals, and is often used to that end, even if unconsciously. Those advocating a new initiative, or those attacking or defending a particular point of view, may invoke the community in support of their case, without making it clear which community they mean, in what sense they refer to it or how far they have established what its opinions or interests are.

Are we stuck with the word?

The suggested set of distinctions may be helpful in clarifying usage. Another approach to the same problem is to try to restrict the use of the term community, on the grounds that it serves only to confuse. This line was taken by Margaret Stacey who argued, in connection with 'community studies' as a method, that community was a 'non-concept', and that it would therefore make more sense to think in terms of 'local social systems' and study those instead[6].

This alternative concept may well be helpful for researchers. A study by Howard Newby and his colleagues of social structure and power in rural Suffolk, for example, focussed on local groupings, their characteristics and their inter-relationships, and thus provided a more useful picture of social reality than might have been expected had the research tried to examine something as vague as the community[7].

But the semantic problem remains for researchers as well as others. Slippery though the notion of community may be, it is certain to continue in general usage, at least for the foreseeable future, whatever efforts might be made to abolish it. There is value in adopting more specific terms for particular purposes, including for some sorts of social research. But for the most part we simply have to accept the word and try to use it as carefully as possible.

The term 'neighbourhood' is somewhat akin to community, being commonly applied to local community in its most local sense. The scale is seldom larger than that of a parish or ward, and it is probably most useful to think of it just as another synonym for community at that level. Although it suffers from some of the slipperiness of community, people are similarly going to continue to use it.

Scope of the study

Part II of this report examines a number of policies and activities with 'community' labels in order to establish what distinguishing features they share, and what, if anything, the community concept means in operation. In looking at different applications, the aim is to identify the 'community' element in each case (for example in what ways does community architecture differ from other architecture?) and to assess its contribution. Some initiatives are examined only briefly, others at greater length. The selection could easily have been different. Outside the obvious candidates, the decisions about what should be in, what out, which treated more fully and which less, were inevitably personal and to some extent arbitrary.

The research includes not only formal community policies of government and other official bodies but also the activities of non-official bodies from regional community arts councils to groups wanting to start community radio stations and from residents' associations to campaigns against hospital closures.

As the last two examples show, the range of initiatives studied has not been confined to those bearing community labels. Local amenity groups, mother and toddler groups, tenants' and residents' associations are all forms of community group, despite not being called that. An official policy which similarly lacks the familiar banner is local government decentralisation.

To add to the semantic difficulties, similar things are being done under both community and non-community labels. For example, the Department of the Environment's Priority Estates Project or the Safe Neighbourhoods Unit (both of which work with local authorities and with tenants on council estates to refurbish and revitalise the estates) could just as well be described as running community housing projects. Different terms are often used within the same general policy. Neighbourhood nursing (to use the terminology of the report of the Community Nursing Review[8]) is obviously as much part of community care as is the community psychiatric service. The lay visitors to police stations scheme could equally well have been called, say, the community visitors scheme, since it is as much concerned with police accountability to the public – or the 'community' – as are police-community consultative committees. Neighbourhood watch –

occasionally called community watch, among other variants – is again part of community policing, being aimed at marshalling the resources of the local community at a highly localised level.

So the study looks more widely than just at activities with explicit community labels. On the other hand some operations that do carry them have been deliberately excluded. One example is the community charge. Although the government has used the label in order to indicate that the charge is paid by members of the community to finance community services, the community element is minimal. (Indeed, the widespread public preference for the term 'poll tax' suggests that there are limits to which the community terminology can be acceptably applied.)

Also excluded are activities which are exclusively directed to profit-making, where again the label – for example community petrol station or community newsagent – is not generally taken up by customers. There is in most community policies and activities a strong element of public service, voluntary endeavour or self help, and that certainly applies to those I have examined.

As all this shows, the subject cannot readily be corseted within a tidy definition; the edges are blurred. But, to sum up, the study covers:

- policies and initiatives,
- official and non-official,
- which are non-profit and
- bear a community label or
- have a kindred interest in neighbourhood or
- are run by local or other indigenous groups
- to further collective ends.

References

1. Royal Commisssion on the Law Relating to Mental Illness and Mental Health, 1954-1957, *Report*, Cmnd. 169, London, HMSO, 1957, p. 245.
2. R. Berthoud and T. Hinton, *Credit Unions in the United Kingdom*, London, Policy Studies Institute, 1989.
3. M. Janowitz and J.D. Kasarda, 'The social construction of local communities', in T. Leggatt (editor), *Sociological Theory and Survey Research*, London, Sage, 1974.
4. R. Williams, *Keywords*, London, Fontana/Croom Helm, 1976.

5. D.J. Smith, 'Research, the community and the police', in P. Willmott (editor), *Policing and the Community*, London, Policy Studies Institute, 1987.
6. M. Stacey, 'The myth of community studies', *British Journal of Sociology*, 20 (2), 1969.
7. H. Newby, C. Bell, D. Rose and P. Saunders, *Property, Paternalism and Power: Class and Control in Rural England*, London, Hutchinson, 1978.
8. Cumberlege Report, *Neighbourhood Nursing – a Focus for Care*, Report of the Community Nursing Review, London, HMSO, 1986.

2 Community in Contemporary Britain

There are two contrasted views about the role of the local community in modern societies such as Britain. One is that the personal mobility and the geographical spread of people's lives make it an anachronism. The other is that on the contrary it is currently alive and healthy. The issue is relevant because attaching the community prefix often takes for granted a sense of common purpose, a capacity to come together to meet common ends or the existence of local networks available to provide help and support. It assumes, in other words, that despite the complexities of the modern world local communities and to some extent dispersed interest communities as well are, or are capable of becoming, attachment communities.

The distinctions introduced in the previous chapter provide a useful starting point in trying to examine the assumption, because everything turns on the kind of community under discussion. In the strictly territorial sense – if a community is defined simply as the population of an identified area – there obviously are local communities in Britain today. It is, however, commonly assumed that local communities mean something to residents in terms of identity and social contacts, and a central question is how far that is true. Likewise, if an interest community is defined as a group of people classified according to a common characteristic such as occupation, religion or shared handicap, then such interest communities clearly exist. But unless the common membership is expressed in sentiment, behaviour or both – unless, in other words, they are at least to some extent attachment communities as well – there is little point in using the community label at all. So the existence and extent of attachment is crucial in examining them.

Scale of local communities

In looking at local territorial communities, a prior question is about their scale. How local is local? As so often, the answer depends on what you mean – which type of local community you are talking about. The fact is that, just as different kinds of community service operate at a variety of local scales, larger or smaller depending on the particular function, residents themselves usually think in terms of a number of local areas, not just one. They have different scales for different purposes. The most local level corresponds to the street or block of flats in which people live and perhaps one or two adjacent ones. This could be called the 'precinct'; it seldom contains more than a few hundred people. At the next scale up, most people think of their local areas as places that make sense according to their own patterns of behaviour locally. Examples are the area within which they can easily walk with very young children, the catchment of a local primary school (because the children's schoolfriends, and the parents of those schoolfriends, are drawn from that area) or, depending on their affiliation, the church parish or political ward.

As these examples indicate, there is a good deal of divergence from person to person about the size and boundaries of such local communities as perceived by them. We do know from surveys, however, that most people's local communities or neighbourhoods of these kinds are areas smaller than wards, with populations of up to 5,000 or so , and we know also that there is often a degree of consensus over specific boundaries, such as railways, major roads and parks[1].

Larger local communities exist, both objectively, for instance as administrative areas, and as perceived subjectively. But unless one stretches the word local beyond its reasonable meaning, the term is not normally applied above the scale of a town or, within a large city, to what is in local government terms a district or borough. A suggested hierarchy of local communities is in Figure 1; it is intended only as a broad indication. The table refers to urban areas, where most of Britain's population live; a comparable scheme could be drawn for rural areas.

Cities as large as Newcastle-upon-Tyne, Birmingham and even London are also territorial communities. They are to some extent attachment communities too; Londoners, for instance, often feel some sense of identity with the metropolis as a whole, and some affection for it. Such larger areas are, however, not local communities in any ordinary meaning of the word.

Figure 1   Hierarchy of urban local communities

Title	Description	Population size
Precinct (or immediate neighbourhood)	Same and adjacent streets/blocks of flats	Several hundred
Neighbourhood	Functional or identifiable larger area, up to about the size of a ward	Between about 3,000 and 10,000
District or small town	Smaller district council area; small town	Between about 25,000 and 75,000
Larger district or town	Larger district council area (incl. metropolitan district council); larger town	Up to about 250,000

The rise of the dispersed community

If, on the face of it, the local community is becoming less important than it has been in the past, there can be no dispute about the growing role of the dispersed community. Advances in communications, and the greater residential and personal mobility they have made possible, have encouraged the development of dispersed social networks and dispersed communities at the expense of local ones.

People increasingly interact with others who do not share local residence with them. In many respects, these developments represent greater choice and variety in people's lives: greater choice over where to live, where to work and whom to mix with; greater variety because specialised interests and tastes can more readily be accommodated within the larger catchment areas (and larger populations) now accessible than they could in the limited territorial communities of the past. These are among the benefits of the modern pattern that has been described as 'community without propinquity'[2].

Relationships with networks of relatives and friends needs to be brought into the picture here, even though they would not normally be described as communities. Such networks, too, can be either local or dispersed. In examining how important such dispersed communities are, and how far they operate as communities of attachment, a distinction has to be made between these networks of relatives or friends on the one hand, and dispersed networks or communities of people whose relationships are weaker.

In contemporary Britain relatives and friends do not necessarily live near each other. On the contrary, most people now belong to kinship and friendship networks that are of substantial importance in their social lives but are geographically dispersed. With modern transport and particularly the private car, with telephones, with enough space to have relatives or friends to stay for weekends or holidays, such dispersed networks can and often do operate effectively. Dispersed kinship networks in particular are important sources of material support and practical help[3].

Members of dispersed kinship networks commonly not only maintain contact with each other and provide mutual services but also have some sense of family identity[4]. Circles of friends, too, as well as keeping in touch, are sometimes aware of their common membership, particularly when a group of them have known each other for a long time. Links with friends, even if the friends are emotionally 'close', are however more often in the form of loose-knit networks, in which most of a person's various friends seldom meet each other[5], and in which there is usually little or no sense of collective identity and no common purpose.

The two main elements of the community of attachment – interaction and sense of identity – can of course operate among people whose relationships with each other are less personal than those with friends and relatives. The importance of these contacts with others, even if trivial, should not be underestimated. If people see themselves as sharing membership with others – whether work colleagues, or people with similar beliefs, political convictions or problems – this helps them, even in the absence of any personal relationships with their fellows, to locate themselves in the wider social structure, and to make sense of their lives in what may otherwise seem a complex and anonymous world.

There are some kinds of grouping in which the social relationships are particularly substantial. Self-help communities – or self-help groups, as they are commonly called – provide one example. Even when geographically dispersed, those who belong often have fairly regular contacts with at least some fellow-members. They also often have a clear sense of attachment, derived from the shared recognition of a common problem and collaborative efforts to do something about it. Other kinds of dispersed community marked by interaction and community sense include those in which the basis is a strongly felt religious, political or campaigning set of beliefs and objectives.

But most of the dispersed interest communities to which people belong are fairly loose groupings. Their membership changes often, people's levels of participation fluctuate, and the reinforcement of continuing contact is lacking. These groupings are, like the majority of circles of friends, more often loose-knit networks than communities of attachment. Examples are an adult education class in photography, or a group of people who come together to play or watch a sport. The variations between dispersed communities in the extent of attachment are explained by differences in their basis and function, and by the relative strength of personal ties and shared benefits.

Trends affecting local community
The general trends which have encouraged dispersal, including greater residential mobility and increased car ownership, have at the same time worked against the locality. Another influence has been the post-war programme of clearance and redevelopment in Britain's towns and cities: this not only broke up existing local networks but usually also redeveloped the old districts in physical forms which made it difficult for people to get to know their new neighbours. Yet another factor has been the post-war rise in the number and proportion of wives working outside the home; although to some extent this change has been made possible by the support of local relatives and friends, who often help in caring for children, the general effect must have been to reduce contacts with people living nearby.

What is more, when men and women are not at work they now spend more time inside their homes than in the past. Their lives are more 'privatised'[6]. This trend has been encouraged by improvements in housing standards, spaciousness and household appliances, and in particular the 'miniaturisation' of equipment[7]. The growth in home-centredness has tended increasingly to polarise people's lives between the home on the one hand and places distant from it on the other.

That is one perspective, one that seems to come down against the view that local communities are now attachment communities to any appreciable degree. But there is a substantial body of research evidence that points the other way. For a start, it is established that even superficial interactions between residents, if regular, encourage some sense of attachment to the locality. As the report of an ethnographic survey in Battersea, London, explained:

> Regular residents...inevitably get to know each other by sight. They meet shopping, standing at the bus-stop or walking in the street, and so learn, over time, the public habits and timetables of people they do not know by name and probably never visit at home. Recognising and being recognised by others creates a sense of belonging[8].

A number of other studies show that the great majority of people, as well as having such knowledge of other residents, have some social relationships with people who live nearby. A sizeable minority in Britain have relatives living close at hand, most have some friends within ten minutes' walk of their home, and nearly all have what they describe as 'friendly' dealings with their neighbours[9].

In addition to such existing links, some current trends are working to strengthen the importance of local ties and local institutions. One such change is demographic – the proportion of older people in the population is increasing, and they are more likely to spend time in their locality than younger people do. In the present economic climate, they are being joined by others who are unemployed, are working shorter hours or have retired early.

Some changes in the economic structure are moving in the same direction. A local territorial community is, amongst other things, a kind of market place in which people produce, exchange, buy and sell goods and services. Despite the general growth in the scale of economic (and other) institutions, there has recently been an increasing re-emphasis on the locality as an economic base. This has so far been clearest in the official and other community schemes deliberately designed to reduce unemployment, but the general official policy of encouraging the development of small firms, which is not an issue that divides the political parties, is also consistent with this development.

Even the home-centredness mentioned earlier is, in its latest phase, likely to increase rather than reduce activity within the local area. A range of technological developments – home computers, word processors, links via optical fibres to commercial services, data banks and information networks – are opening the way to a regeneration of cottage industry in new forms. Meanwhile, changes in the relationships between men and women are reinforcing the switch to the home as a place of paid work. Although most of the time of the new homeworkers will inevitably be spent inside the homes, they are likely to play more of a part in the locality than if they worked elsewhere.

Variations in local community

The impact of these various changes – some weakening localities, others strengthening them – has differed from area to area. Places vary in the number and strength of local ties and in the degree of local identity or community sense; some places are therefore communities of attachment to a greater degree than others. Patterns differ, too, for different kinds of people, even in the same place.

The research evidence shows which characteristics of places – and of people – have most influence on the extent of local inter-relationships and local identity[10]. Places are more likely to be attachment communities when the following conditions apply.

- When there has been relative population stability, and thus large proportions of people have had lengthy continuous residence in the area.
- When kin live in the area.
- When many people work in a local industry.
- When people are alike in social class and income, or share membership of a particular minority.
- When a large proportion of local people have the specific social skills, and the appropriate values, to get to know others quickly.
- When there are many locally-based organisations.
- When a place or its residents are under an external threat, particularly when this results in the creation of local campaigning organisations (though this may be a more temporary effect than the others).
- When physical layout and design encourage rather than discourage casual neighbourly meetings and a sense of separate physical identity.
- When a place is particularly isolated.

In terms of the residents, the following kinds of people more often develop attachment to their local territorial community.

- Those, again, who have the relevant skills and values including a readiness to join a local organisation – all of which have so far been more common among middle-class people.
- Those who have young children (especially if the mother is not in full-time work outside the home and has no car) and those who are elderly (again, especially if they have no car).
- Those whose family background, past experience or temperament predispose them to be sociable.

Many of these characteristics of places or people fall into one or other of two distinct categories. The first set might be described as the 'traditional' bases of solidarity and local interaction: long residence, having kin locally and being relatively constrained by the lack of private transport. These characteristics have in the past been more common in working-class districts than others. They help to encourage the growth of local relationships and loyalties among residents without deliberate efforts by local people themselves.

The second set by contrast depends on the disposition and actions of people themselves: the application of social skills in making friends nearby, and the readiness to do so: the creation of local campaigns against actual or potential external threats; the existence of many local organisations. Such means, it is clear, have in the past been more often used by middle-class people, and have therefore been more important in middle-class areas than others.

This distinction – based on the modes by which communities of attachment are developed – is useful in assessing how local community stands today. Each mode corresponds to a distinctive style of attachment community – the traditional and the non-traditional – and an obvious question is about the relative importance of each. There are in this two-fold distinction some affinities to that made by Philip Abrams between what he called, respectively, the traditional community (or neighbourhood) and new neighbourhoodism. The first was characterised by 'The densely woven world of kin, neighbours, friends and co-workers, highly localised and strongly caring within the confines of quite tightly defined relationships, above all the relationships of kinship'. The second depended on 'organisational skills and ingenious organisational devices...used in attempts to mobilise old and new residents alike in order to protect amenities, enhance resources and, to a greater or lesser degree, wrench control of the local milieu from outside authorities and vest it in local hands'[11].

It can be argued that in his description of the new style of local territorial community, Abrams exaggerated the importance of what he called 'political or quasi-political action'. That is obviously one element, but others include deliberately setting out to make new friends and joining local organisations (not just campaigning ones). However, if it is modified to include these further components, the Abrams distinction provides two useful contrasted models.

In practice, few if any places correspond precisely to one or the other. In the most traditional community there are usually some newcomers, lacking local kin and knowing few, if any, residents; this was true even of the close-knit community of Bethnal Green in the 1950s[12]. Likewise, although suburban Woodford at the same date was predominantly the new kind of community, some of its residents had lived there a long time and some had relatives nearby – and such people were by no means confined to the working classes[13]. It is a matter of balance, some districts being predominantly traditional in style, some predominantly new, and others a more complex blend.

It is clear that there are now more communities in which attachments have been built up in the new ways, and those communities which are still substantially traditional are less so than in the past. More places, for more residents, are near the 'new' end of the spectrum rather than the 'traditional'.

Conclusions

It is not true, as some people have supposed, that new communities cannot be attachment communities. But the decline of the traditional working-class community does mean that, in the course of this century at least, there has been a long-term reduction in the number and proportion of places with dense local networks and a strong sense of local solidarity. The newer styles for developing community ties work well enough for their purpose, for most people, but the outcome is more attenuated, less all-embracing than the traditional pattern. It also excludes those who, because they are too timorous or lack relevant experience, do not find it easy to establish new relationships.

At the same time it is clear from the research evidence that the overwhelming majority of people have reasonably 'friendly' (if often superficial) social contacts with neighbours, that most have some personal friends living locally and that many have some relatives within reach. If the criterion is the experience of the majority of residents, most districts in Britain exhibit what might be described as at least a moderate degree of local interaction. Less is known about the sense of local identity. The last national study on this was a 'community attitudes survey' in England (excluding Greater London) in 1967, when nearly four people out of every five reported some feeling of attachment to their 'home' community area[14]. Local surveys at around the same date or a few years later mostly had similar results, exceptions being in inner city areas such as Lambeth in 1973 and Southwark in 1975, where only 35 per cent and 40 per cent respectively responded positively to roughly comparable questions[15]. If the national survey were repeated now the proportions might be different from those in 1967, and would certainly show variations between places, with inner city areas tending to score low. But it seems unlikely that British society as a whole has changed so much in two decades that the general picture would be dramatically reversed. Apart from anything else, such a result would contradict the research findings on the links between neighbours, including those from a national survey in 1982[16]. So it seems likely that it remains true that for most people, and therefore most places, there is some sense – often vague and relatively weak – of local attachment to place.

Thus in terms both of social relationships and local identity most localities in present-day Britain, for most of their residents, have something of the character of a community of attachment. At the local scale, territorial communities are seldom just that and nothing more.

The general pattern does not, however, correspond to a mosaic of small identifiable local communities. Although some discrete geographical areas constitute physically identifiable communities at a relatively small scale – most villages, for example, and a few urban areas – at local levels few places have clearly defined boundaries about which residents agree.

One consequence of the current structure of relationships and attachments is that most people now have more choice about how fully they will participate in their residential community. They can decide to have nothing to do with their neighbours or with local affairs; or they can choose to become heavily engaged in their locality. This voluntary character of local attachment has been summed up well in the term 'community of limited liability'[17].

The rise of dispersed social networks and dispersed communities of interest has meant that, to a greater extent than in the past, local attachments now constitute only one part of social life among others.

Most residents look beyond their local community for many of their social relationships, often including some of those most important to them. Local ties are weaker than they have historically been, because they overlap much less often than they used to with other ties, of kinship, friendship, work, leisure and other interests. The multiplicity of strands which reinforce local social relationships have been separating out since the Industrial Revolution, the process having been accelerated by developments in transport and communications – and particularly, over the last four decades, by the spread in car ownership.

Two conclusions can be drawn from this chapter. The first is that there is some basis on which to build community-oriented policies. Britain is made up of communities, both territorial and interest, which constitute a soil – more fertile in some places than others – in which community activities can and do develop. The second conclusion is that most places and most interest groups are attachment communities to only a limited extent.

References

1. On the extent of disagreement and agreement and on scale, see P. Willmott, 'Social research in new communities', *Journal of the American Institute of Planners*, 33 (5), 1967 and Royal Commission on Local Government in England, 'Representation and community', Appendix 7, *Research Appendices*, Vol. III, Cmnd. 4040-II, London, HMSO, 1969.
2. M. M. Webber, 'Order and diversity: community without propinquity', in Lowdon Wingo Jnr (editor), *Cities and Space*, Baltimore, John Hopkins, 1964.
3. See P. Willmott, Chapters II and III, *Social Networks, Informal Care and Public Policy*, London, Policy Studies Institute, 1986.
4. Ibid., Chapter II.
5. A recent survey in a north London suburb found that, of all the friends of members of the sample, about a third knew each other; the proportion was particularly low – about a quarter – among people with higher or further education. See Chapter V of P. Willmott, *Friendship Networks and Social Support*, London, Policy Studies Institute, 1987.
6. J.H. Goldthorpe, D. Lockwood, F. Bechhofer and J. Platt, *The Affluent Worker in the Class Structure*, London, Cambridge University Press, 1969.

7. M. Young and P. Willmott, *The Symmetrical Family*, London, Routledge and Kegan Paul, 1973.
8. S. Wallman, *Eight London Households*, London Tavistock, 1984.
9. See the research reviewed in Chapters IV and VI in P. Willmott, 1986, op.cit.
10. See P. Willmott, ibid., pp.90-95.
11. M. Bulmer, *Neighbours: the Work of Philip Abrams*, Cambridge, Cambridge University Press, 1986.
12. M. Young and P. Willmott, *Family and Kinship in East London*, London, Routledge and Kegan Paul, 1957.
13. P. Willmott and M. Young, *Family and Class in a London Suburb*, London, Routledge and Kegan Paul, 1960.
14. Royal Commission on Local Government in England, op.cit.
15. G. Shankland, P. Willmott and D. Jordan, *Inner London: Policies for Dispersal and Balance*, Final report of the Lambeth Inner Area Study, London, HMSO, 1977; P. Prescott-Clarke and B. Hedges, *Living in Southwark*, London, Social and Community Planning Research, 1976.
16. Market Opinion and Research International (MORI), *Neighbours: Computer Tables*, London, MORI (duplicated), 1982.
17. M. Janowitz and G.D. Suttles, 'The social ecology of citizenship' in R.C. Sarri and Y. Hasenfield (editors), *The Management of Human Services*, New York, Columbia University Press, 1978.

3   Patterns of Community Activity

The aim of this chapter is to examine how far a pattern or set of patterns can be discerned in the community initiatives introduced and developed in Britain in recent years.

Areas and populations

As part of the process of looking for similarities and differences, I look first at the areas and populations covered. For a start some community initiatives are local and small scale, while others cover large geographical areas and populations.

The scale is affected by the origin of the initiative – by whether the local area is, for example, determined by an official service or by a small group, with the former areas being generally larger than the latter. Community Health Councils, for instance, which were launched by central government, usually cover the same area as their District Health Authorities, with populations of between about 90,000 and 900,000; Community Councils in Scotland serve populations of between about 50,000 and 100,000; and police-community consultative committees in England and Wales serve populations of between about 60,000 and 150,00 people. Again, towns and cities the size of Bath (80,000), Luton (160,000) and York (100,000) and even Bristol (400,000) and Sheffield (500,000), for instance, have some town-wide community activities; and in London and other metropolitan areas there are many community schemes at borough or district level.

Most indigenous community schemes operate at a smaller scale than these. Residents' and tenants' associations cover a hundred or several hundred households and are limited to a few streets or a small housing estate. Play groups and mother and toddler groups have fewer participants, but operate in similar sized geographical catchment areas. Other indigenous schemes may range in scale up to the equivalent of a ward, which have average populations of about 5,000 but as many as 15,000 or more people in some urban areas. The community areas used by voluntary organisations, community arts projects and the like can vary widely.

Some community activities do not operate at a local scale at all, and in this sense their catchment area is unusually large. This applies particularly to those self-help groups which cater for people with rare illnesses or problem who are consequently more dispersed geographically. For instance, parents whose children have Downs syndrome are relatively few in number in the general population, so that their groups need to operate on a city-wide or regional basis. But these are exceptions to the general run of indigenous community-style activities.

In selecting an area of operation, local groups such as residents' associations, mother and toddler groups and play groups choose an area which is appropriate in size and boundaries (if any) for the activity in question. Officially determined services, however, such as parts of the health service and local authority social services, set out to create manageable elements; they do not usually choose areas on the grounds that they make sense or are particularly convenient for users.

A weakness of the usual official approach is that the areas selected are not always co-terminous with each other, even when the various services need to collaborate closely, as for example with community care, and differences have been shown to cause confusion and make life difficult for both clients and workers in the various services[1]. There have been some official moves to encourage common boundaries for health services, social services and social security, but the obstacles are great – partly for practical reasons, partly because of institutional resistance to change – and little progress has so far been made.

Prevalence
Community initiatives also differ in what might be called their prevalence: the number of separate operations or schemes, or the total numbers of people affected.

The numbers of most official schemes can be established. For example, all the 369 district councils and the 201 district health councils in England and Wales are operating some form of community care; all the 43 police forces in England and Wales have some form of community policing, with beat policemen, crime prevention panels and consultative committees, and at the end of 1988 there were 64,000 neighbourhood watch schemes; in 1986 Wales had 289 community councils and Scotland 1,342.

In terms of the numbers of schemes, community policing and community care dominate among official initiatives, but the two of them affect very different total numbers of people. Three and a quarter million households in England and Wales belong (at least nominally) to neighbourhood watch schemes – that is more than one household in every six. Probably only about one person in 20 is in contact with community care services.

It is difficult to estimate the numbers of indigenous community groups or of the people in them, but the numbers of local groups affiliated to their respective national bodies include, for example, about 2,000 tenants' associations, 1,200 community 'organisations' (community associations and the like), and 18,500 play groups. In most community groups the proportion of active, as distinct from nominal, members may be between about one in ten and one in 20.

Origins of initiatives

As I have indicated, the origins of community initiatives – where the initial idea and the drive came from – can range from central government at one extreme to a handful of local residents at the other. A useful distinction in exploring such differences is between what are sometimes described as top-down activities and bottom-up activities.

Community care is a top-down policy, originating with central government, as is community policing. Other central government initiatives are Community Health Councils and Community Councils in Scotland and Wales. Community education is encouraged by the Department of Education and Science in new design schemes, and is pursued explicitly by many local education authorities. Local authority decentralisation is also top-down.

Indigenous community groups are manifestly bottom-up. A collection of interested residents may, for example, launch a residents' association, a play school, a campaign against a motorway or against the proposed closure of a school or hospital, and groups of people with particular illnesses or problems get together to create a self-help group.

In practice there is considerable interdependence and interaction between top-down and bottom-up schemes. Not only may a top-down initiative depend for its implementation on voluntary, bottom-up bodies; it may also be part of official policy to encourage the development of indigenous activity so that community groups and informal social networks can make their contribution. For example, although the official policy of community care originated with central government, it requires the collaboration not only of local authorities, district health authorities and other statutory agencies but also of voluntary organisations and community groups and even more of the relatives, friends and neighbours who act as informal carers. Likewise, the Home Office encourages community policing, where the various police forces have responsibility for most of the specific measures, such as beat policing, neighbourhood watch and consultative committees. In practice much of the implementation of these measures is devolved to police subdivisions, which in their turn depend to some extent on the initiatives of local residents, for example in starting up neighbourhood watch schemes. So, even if the origins are top-down, the development of bottom-up initiatives, in which local people play a crucial part, may well be essential to success.

Between the extremes of the top-down official policy and the bottom-up indigenous initiative is a range of schemes originated by intermediate agencies or groups of enthusiasts. The initiators seek to encourage and support individual people or local organisations to come together for a particular community project or campaign. Examples of such initiators include national, regional or local voluntary bodies which promote community arts or community health projects; firms which join other firms (for example, through Business in the Community schemes) to provide services to local people or to create a local enterprise agency; actors or producers who set up a community theatre; and existing groups seeking to set up a community association or community centre to serve a number of local organisations. The initiators are sometimes professional community workers, whose job it is to encourage local collaborative activities of these kinds.

One way of looking at the relationship between bottom-up, intermediate and top-down community initiatives in a local setting is shown in Figure 2, which presents a modified version of a framework suggested by Gabriel Chanin of the Community Projects Foundation[2]. The four columns represent, in a simplified form, four elements at work within local communities and relevant to community initiatives, going from the most informal and indigenous activities in the extreme left-hand column to the most official and institutionally-inspired in the extreme right-hand column.

Figure 2   Types of localised community initiative

Neighbourhood life	Community action (bottom-up)	Community development (top-down or intermediate)	Implementation of official community policies (top-down)
Daily activities taking place without any formal organisation in local communities (Examples: social contacts and mutual aid among neighbours, local friends, and local relatives)	Indigenous activities, organised by local people (Examples: playgroup, protest group, residents' association)	Efforts involving community workers, other professionals and enthusiasts (Examples: supporting indigenous community action, promoting community arts and community centres)	Measures by institutions to implement policies and promote collaboration (Examples: neighbourhood watch, community care)

Although community initiatives can be broadly categorised as top-down, bottom-up or intermediate, once the activity is launched things usually become more complicated, as is illustrated by the examples of official policies mentioned earlier. As a result, some types of activity are too complex to fit neatly into the three-fold schema. Community architecture, for instance, though pioneered by voluntary organisations and independent architects, has been formally endorsed and supported by central government, but local schemes are in practice launched by local authorities, housing associations and other landlords. Community workers can operate in a top-down, bottom-up or intermediate fashion, whether employed by a public or voluntary body.

A common pattern is for bottom-up community projects to be taken over in time by official, top-down bodies. A prevalent reason is that the official organisation has been called upon for funding and, wishing to ensure accountability for its expenditure, becomes involved in direction and management. In such cases the initiators, anxious for the project to continue, may come to feel that they have to accept what some of them see as undue interference or even a corruption of the original vision. An example might be a local community association and its community centre which, receiving substantial financial support from the local authority, eventually come to be (as the founders see it) 'taken over' by the council, with the result that some of the users may feel that the centre's independence and freedom have been sacrificed.

Objectives
Distinctions can also be drawn between various initiatives in terms of their aims or objectives. Objectives are not, of course, the same as achievements; indeed some of the most important questions, particularly about official policies such as community care and community policing, are about how far they succeed in meeting their avowed aims. This is taken up in the next chapter. But it is still useful to classify initiatives in terms of what they are trying to do.

A list of objectives, with examples under each heading, is given in Figure 3. As the list shows, community initiatives often have more than one objective in the list. Community care policies are intended to provide locally accessible services and also to mesh them with informal forms of support. Local government decentralisation often has the twin aims of decentralising services and sharing power more widely. Many community groups share two or more of the last three objectives in the list. A residents' association or a self-help group is likely to see its main tasks as to represent its members, exert pressure to improve their conditions or resist what are seen as deleterious changes, and often also provide some services on a mutual basis or for members with special needs.

In addition to the objectives with which they were established, community measures may well have consequences, including beneficial ones, that develop as the schemes develop. Those consequences may have been intended or not intended by the organisers or participants. Community groups, for example, seldom set out with the explicit aim of promoting social mixing between those who take part, yet all do so. Some, once established, do it more or less deliberately, as when a tenants' association organises social evenings; more commonly, the social contacts – and the neighbourly relationships and, sometimes, close personal friendships that develop as a result – are not planned but are by-products of the group's operations.

Figure 3   Objectives of community initiatives

Objective	Examples
Devolution of services	Community policing, community care local government decentralisation
Linking formal services with informal	Community policing, community care community social work
Consultation, devolution of power	Community Health Councils, local government decentralisation community architecture
Provide local jobs and serve locality	Community industry, Business in the Community community insulation projects
Increase political awareness/skills	Local government decentralisation some community work, community organisations
Enrich lives, develop capacities	Community arts, community education, community theatre
Increase sense of community	Community organisations, some community groups
Improve/preserve conditions	Some community work, some community groups (Examples: protests against school/ hospital closures, campaigns for by-passes/clinics)
Represent members/local people	Tenants' associations, residents associations, self-help groups
Provide services to members/ others	Play schools, mother and toddler groups, self-help groups

An official policy – community policing – provides an example of this process. As reported in Chapter 8, researchers studying the working of two neighbourhood watch schemes in London found that they had no measureable impact on the level of reported crime, but the members said that friendly relationships with each other had increased because of their contacts in the schemes.

The objectives of initiatives have some relationship to their origins. The examples cited as aiming for 'the devolution of services' are, for instance, all official policies. The relationship between the origins and objectives if community iniatives is shown in Figure 4.

Figure 4   Origins of community initiatives and types of objective

	Top-down	Intermediate	Bottom-up
Delivery of services	✓		
Mesh formal/informal Consultation/devolution	✓		
Provide local jobs/ serve locality	✓	✓	
Increase political awareness/ skills		✓	
Enrich lives/develop capacities		✓	
Increase sense of community		✓	
Improve/preserve conditions		✓	✓
Represent members/ local people			✓
Provide services to members/ others			✓

The picture presented here is only a broad guide. Some activities fit less readily than indicated, and it should be borne in mind that at this stage the focus is on aims, not on what actually happens in practice. But there are some clear patterns. Top-down initiatives are largely directed to improving the quality of people's lives, through better services and the like, through more effective collaboration between formal and informal activity; and they often also seek to involve people more fully through consultation or some devolution of decisions. Bottom-up initiatives are mainly concerned with representing people's views and interests, with campaigning and with self-help. The objectives of intermediately-originated initiatives are often less clear-cut than either of the others, but the general flavour is altruistic or, as a critic might say, paternalistic.

A general trend?
The chapter so far has identified some points of similarity and difference, and some common patterns, in community initiatives. But

there remains the question of whether or not these initiatives form part of a general trend.

There has certainly been a shift of popular feeling in Britain against centralised institutions. Despite the noble aspirations of the post-war welfare state, in practice it often seemed bureaucratic and insensitive to people's needs. Until about the late 1960s, centralisation was the unchallenged order of the day. Policemen were taken off the beat. Local authority areas were greatly enlarged, making their councils less accessible than anywhere else in the Western world. Resident caretakers were replaced, on grounds of cost-effectivess, by faceless men in overalls driving about in vans. In the private sector large corporations and the multi-nationals in particular became ever more dominant.

As a result of all this there was from about the mid-1960s a reaction against the growth in the scale and remoteness of institutions, public and private. By the early 1980s, the Barclay Report, in proposing the development of community social work, saw that proposal as part of a broader tendency, one that it described as 'a very general movement away from centralism and towards a belief in ordinary people'[3].

Barclay summed up a perspective that policy-makers and managers in different fields had come increasingly to share. The 1957 Royal Commission on mental illness and what we would now call mental handicap, whose recommendations were embodied in the 1959 Mental Health Act, was the first sign of movement. At first slowly, and then with growing momentum, the community idea spread in the public services, along with the recognition that the community, in the sense of local people acting as carers, unofficial policemen and the like, might save money, or at least mean that it could be spent to better effect. In private and public sectors alike, the belief grew, too, that decentralised administration made for more effective management.

As David Donnison has argued, politicians and policy-makers changed their minds partly because they saw community-based activities as offering new solutions to problems 'which defeated conventional services operating in conventional ways'. He gave some examples:

> The police, investigated by Lord Scarman after disturbances which drove them off the Brixton streets, are adopting his proposals for community liaison groups and other initiatives which are designed to elicit support from the public... Medical services have increasingly come to accept the view...that their most important

task is not to cure disease but to help citizens take more care of their own health... Housing authorities have...turned increasingly to housing management cooperatives, community ownership schemes and other locally-based forms of collective action to help them tackle these problems[4].

The point is borne out in several of the chapters in Part II of this report. I argue in Chapter 6 that to some extent local government politicians and managers turned to decentralisation to help deal with the excessive scale of local authorities and the public criticism of much public housing management; in Chapter 8 that the Home Office and senior police officers saw community policing as a way out of a set of new problems; and in Chapter 9 that some thoughful architects, recognising the low reputation of their profession after the high-rise disasters of the post-war years, tried to find an acceptable new role for themselves.

Another reason for the trend is suggested by the American sociologist Peter Berger. He argues that, in view of the dichotomy in modern life between large and complex institutions on the one hand and the 'private sphere' on the other, people increasingly need intermediate institutions if they are to make sense of their lives and feel members of human society. These mediating structures 'stand between the individual in his private sphere and the large institutions of the public sphere', examples being voluntary organisations, churches and local community groups. They are as essential to the society as to individual people because, without them, there could be no effective political or social order[5].

The development of community policies and initiatives can be seen as part of a growing understanding of their role as mediating structures, though Berger's analysis and language are seldom invoked. Community groupings and activities are seen as important partly because there is a widening recognition that mediating structures are increasingly necessary. This applies most clearly to local territorial communities, as illustrated by community architecture, community policing and community care. But mediating structures do not have to be local. The same arguments apply to interest communities that are not locally-based as well as those that are.

The general shift identified by the Barclay report – the 'movement away from centralism and towards a belief in ordinary people' – is sometimes expressed in terms other than community, such as 'participation', 'empowerment' or 'citizenship'. Two fundamental aims are increasingly recognised as worthwhile objectives of policy. The first is to help people to come together in meeting their needs and tackling common problems. The second is for public services to strengthen voluntary and informal structures and to work with rather than against them.

This chapter, to conclude, has looked at similarities and differences in community initiatives, and has identified some of the patterns in them. It has also shown that, notwithstanding all the variations, the various threads – some distinctively British, some of wider application – form part of a general trend or movement.

References

1. G. Shankland, P. Willmott and D. Jordan, *Inner London: Policies for Dispersal and Balance*, Final Report of the Lambeth Inner Area Study, London, HMSO, 1977, Chapter 9.
2. Gabriel Chanin, of the Community Projects Foundation, in a paper given at a seminar organised by the Foundation in 1988.
3. Barclay Report, *Social Workers: their Role and Tasks*, London, Bedford Square Press for National Institute of Social Work, 1982, p. 204.
4. D. Donnison, 'Social policy and the community' in M. Bulmer, J. Lewis and D. Piachaud (editors), *The Goals of Social Policy*, London, Unwin Hyman, 1989.
5. P. Berger, *Facing Up to Modernity*, New York, Basic Books, 1977.

4   The Value of Community Initiatives

This chapter, which concludes Part I of the report, draws upon the previous chapters and also upon the case studies in Part II. There can be little disagreement about the objectives of the general trend and of most community initiatives. The question is how usefully, in practice, the community idea contributes to public policy.

Some limitations

It is clearly a mistake to expect community initiatives to transform Britain into a multitude of harmonious utopias. There probably never has been a 'golden age' of the kind sometimes evoked, and even if there had, it would not be possible to return to it or anything like it. Modern society – with its large institutions, world-wide communications and dispersed social networks – is too different for that to be possible.

In particular, to refer to the typology introduced in the introductory chapter, the modern territorial community is less of an attachment community than is sometimes assumed. Community policing can, through neighbourhood watch schemes, bring the residents of a few streets or blocks of flats together to collaborate with the police in combatting crime. Tenants can take on substantial responsibility for managing their own estates and parents for managing their children's schools. These examples are highly localised and are based on clear common interests. But the concept of community is often applied in cases where an effective community, in the attachment sense, hardly exists. For example, community care is discussed as if 'the community' can in some way care for its frail elderly residents and its severely handicapped members, an assumption which is manifestly false.

The fact is that, whatever things might have been like in the past, people's attachment to their local community is nowadays usually rather tenuous. As Chapter 2 pointed out, most people probably feel some sense of identity with their locality. But that sense is seldom very strong and residents are for the most part vague about the geographical boundaries of 'their' community. Beyond that, insofar as people have attachments to their fellow-residents, these are links to particular people built on specific ties – ties to relatives, to immediate neighbours, to fellow churchgoers, to those who use the same pub or social club, to fellow footballers, darts players or anglers, to the fellow members of other locally-based interest communities – including, as mentioned earlier, the parents of children at the same school or the residents of the same housing estate.

When a majority of people have a multiplicity of such local ties, there can be said to be a strong local community of attachment. But in the modern world that is rare. It is a mistake to base policy on the belief that, except in limited instances, local community exists today in any general sense as a potential resource, waiting to be tapped.

Another basic error in much thinking about community is to do with consensus and conflict. Up to the 1970s those who advocated community measures commonly believed that local people had much the same basic interests and values as each other. This assumption of consensus characterised the 1969 Skeffington Report, which said for example 'People should be able to say what kind of community they want'[1]. Nationally, too, there was in that Butskellite era a widespread assumption that, despite some differences of emphasis, most people not only wanted the same things – continuing economic growth, a rising personal standard of living, better educational opportunities for their children – but were also broadly agreed about how to achieve them.

Most people now recognise that, both locally and on a larger canvas, different groups can have conflicting interests – a point that comes out clearly in the discussion about community policing in Chapter 8. The only sensible way to handle such conflicts is through what Andrew Thornley calls 'bargaining'. Thornley argues that where there are conflicting interests the right course is to seek some kind of rational 'negotiation' between them, although such a resolution of differences cannot, of course, always be successfully achieved[2].

A final myth is about the impact of community initiatives upon poverty. It was once supposed that local community activity could help to reduce poverty. But poverty is mainly a function of low income and of the distribution of wealth, income and opportunities. Community development projects, community action programmes and the like can help some individual participants to develop their capacities and perhaps move out of poverty, but the belief that such small-scale schemes could have any fundamental impact on social and economic structures has long been exposed as mistaken[3].

Problems of application

Apart from these limitations of community initiatives, the important question is how they work in practice. The aims may for the most part be laudable enough, but an assessment needs to be made of how often, and to what extent, the reality matches the aspiration.

Time and again the case studies which form Part II of this report point to the same discouraging conclusion. There are many examples of success, of measureable achievement. But it is also clear that community policies often fail to meet their objectives at all fully. What is called community care may sometimes result in patients or elderly people being discharged to a non-caring 'community'. Beat policemen are thin on the ground; there are weaknesses in police-community consultative arrangements; neighbourhood watch schemes may have less impact than hoped. Community architecture has its limitations. And so on.

In trying to make an evaluation, we need first of all to be clear what success means for different kinds of community activity. The distinction between top-down and bottom-up initiatives is helpful here. By and large, top-down community measures seek to reach down and work with citizens, whereas bottom-up initiatives seek to reach up, expressing people's views to officialdom, or they work sideways, with people providing services for themselves or each other.

Manifestly, success means different things in the two cases. With top-down policies, success means delivering services (for example, community care or policing) more effectively or it means drawing upon people's own resources to complement official provision (again of community care, for example, or of policing in their neighbourhood). With bottom-up or intermediate activities, on the other hand, the criterion is how far people's lives are enriched or their conditions improved as a result of their participation.

In general there is little need to doubt the resilience of bottom-up and intermediate expressions of the community idea. People have been creating their own groupings over the centuries, even if, in response to the complexity of modern societies, the scale and the diversity of these activities have become greater than in the past. Where such activities interact with official bodies, some attention needs to be given to ensure the fitness of particular community groups for responsibility, and some of the issues facing indigenous groups are discussed in Chapter 5. But by and large they can be left to themselves. The main interest is in what can be done by way of official policy.

One problem affecting local government decentralisation, community architecture and other developments is how to strike the right balance in devolving power to local people. If people are consulted – in other words, simply asked for their views – this can be dismissed as mere 'tokenism'. The result may be to generate cynicism about official intentions. But if a substantial degree of decision making is devolved, this may lead to muddle and delays, and what is decided by local people may anyway go against a broader-based policy determined by a constitutionally elected body.

There are problems, too, in devolving decisions to local officers or officials. Again the decisions taken on the spot may not mesh with official policies and priorities. If community social workers operating in local 'patches' respond to social problems as presented to them by the most articulate or most demanding residents, they may ignore the council's policy priorities, for example to keep infirm elderly people out of hospital.

What is done may also undermine the principle of equity or weaken the rule of law. This might happen, for example, when a locally-based police officer tried to head off an incipient riot by dealing 'flexibly', in the approved 'community policing' manner, with an offender. What seemed to him like a sensible pragmatic move to cool things down by not making too much of a particular misdemeanor might later be judged by his senior officers or by another group of local citizens – another section of the community – to have condoned what was done, treating it too lightly or applying different rules to some citizens than to others.

For both top-down policies and bottom-up activities, problems can arise from the unwillingness of most people to give much of their free time to community participation. Most of us, most of the time, are too concerned with our own lives and those of our families to want to devote much energy to community service or activity. The result is that, as community architects and community police officers have found, the agents of policy cannot always be sure how far community representatives represent 'community' views or interests. From the bottom-up point of view, some citizens may feel their views or interests are neglected or misrepresented.

Examples of the difficulty are the role of 'politically committed' community activists in London described by Barry Knight and Ruth Hayes in their study cited in Chapter 5[4], and the observation by a Home Office Local Radio Working Party in 1980 that the demand for community radio came mainly from potential programme makers 'rather than from the public'[5]. Public authorities and others working with, or responding to, community representatives need to be clear whom those representatives actually represent.

Facing the problems
Such problems are not in themselves grave enough to undermine the general case for community policies. Some of the difficulties can, with experience and sensitivity, be resolved or at least eased by devising proper procedures, checks and balances. But finding such solutions depends on a willingness to face the problems honestly, and that is not always easily done.

The main concerns are clear – worries about the lack of practical content to broadly-stated aims, a failure to match resources to aspirations, a failure of practice to match promises. The main message is the need to be alive to the dangers of rhetoric. About any specific policy or programme with a community (or similar) label the following are among the questions that need to be posed.

- To what extent have those responsible for the policy or programme explained the case for it?
- On what evidence – or assumptions – is the policy based?
- How far have those responsible explained how success would be measured?
- What attempts have been made to assess how far the policy or programme is succeeding – has succeeded – in meeting its aims?
- In the light of such assessments, what are the costs – financial and non-financial – of the policy or programme, as compared with other ways of doing things? Apart from its assumed advantages, what disadvantages does it have, what new problems does it raise?

- What resources are the authorities concerned committing – and what are they prepared to commit – in support of the policy? This is the question which Sir Roy Griffiths[6] has urged the government to answer about community care (see Chapter 7).

At present such questions are seldom asked and less often answered. Those responsible for policy naturally find life easier if they are ignored. But if this happens the rest of us cannot be clear about the reasoning behind a particular policy or about the extent to which it is meeting its objectives.

In conclusion

The community trend has already brought benefits. Some people with mental handicaps are living richer lives, in small group homes and the like, than they previously did in large institutions. Many elderly people who would otherwise have been in hospital are being cared for in their own homes, through a combination of formal and informal support. Many residents are getting together with each other and with the police in efforts to reduce crime. Some tenants have more say about the design and management of their estates. In some local areas council services are being delivered more effectively than in the past, and residents have a better chance to express their views about council policies that affect them.

These and many other developments are undoubtedly improving people's lives. And what is happening is part of a general tendency to take people's interests into account, to give them more say, to collaborate with them.

Yet many obstacles and problems remain. Those responsible for community policies, from the government down, need to be aware of the limitations of community initiatives, of what such measures can never hope to do in a complex modern society like our own, as well as what with wise and sensitive management they might succeed in doing. They need to recognise the practical problems of application touched on in this chapter and discussed more fully in the case studies, to acknowledge the difficulties and to set out to overcome them more successfully than they have done, for the most part, to date.

If these things can be done, the trend to community policy will prove to be an immensely valuable contribution to British life, and will be universally welcomed. Otherwise the experience must end in disappointment and public disillusion.

References

1. Skeffington Report, *People and Planning*, Report of the Committee on Public Participation in Planning, London, HMSO, 1969.
2. A. Thornley, 'Theoretical perspectives on planning participation', *Progress and Planning*, 7 (1), 1977.
3. See for example P. Marris and M. Rein, *Dilemmas of Social Reform*, London, Routledge and Kegan Paul, 1967 on the United States; National Community Development Project, *Inter-Project Report*, London, Community Development Project Information and Intelligence Unit, 1974 and J. Higgins, *The Poverty Business: Britain and America*, Oxford, Basil Blackwell, 1978 on Britain.
4. B. Knight and R. Hayes, *Self-Help in the Inner City*, London, London Voluntary Service Council, 1981.
5. Home Office Local Radio Working Party, *Third Report*, London, Home Office, 1980.
6. Griffiths Report, *Community Care: Agenda for Action*, A Report to the Secretary of State for Social Services by Sir Roy Griffiths, London, HMSO, 1988.

PART II   THE CASE STUDIES

5 Community Groups and Projects

The second part of this report is composed of case studies. This and the next four chapters examine particular examples in some depth, and a final chapter contains brief reviews of eight further examples.

In selecting the five cases for more intensive study, two criteria have been used. The first is the field of policy in which broader community initiatives fall. Four of the examples cover major areas of public policy: local government (decentralisation); social services and health (community care); law and order (community policing); housing and town planning (community architecture). Community groups and projects, the subjects of this chapter, do not fit neatly into the scheme, because they can be concerned with almost any aspect of collective life.

The second criterion is the extent to which the particular initiatives results from central as against local decisions. The examples have been chosen to represent contrasted sources of origin. Community groups and projects are started in diverse ways, most commonly by a handful of local residents, sometimes by community workers or a local committee and sometimes by a voluntary organisation or even a statutory one. Local government decentralisation is taking place wholly as a result of the decisions of local authorities themselves. Community care is a policy which originated with central government. Community policing, though resulting in part from Home Office encouragement, depends upon action by the various police forces. Community architecture depends on the decisions of a range of local bodies, including housing cooperatives, housing associations and local authorities.

Aims and scale

Community groups cover a wide range, and most of them do not bear that label. They include residents' or tenants' associations, play groups, mother and toddler groups, family centres, amenity groups, local protest or pressure groups and all types of self-help group. It is impossible even to estimate the total number of community groups in Britain, but there are tens of thousands of them at any one time. Some develop and become permanent, or go on to spawn new groups or projects. Others are created to meet what is seen as a particular need and then, after success or failure, fatigue or disenchantment, come to an end. Some continue to struggle on long after they have outlived their usefulness.

Rather similar paths are followed by some so-called community projects. The total number of community projects has increased substantially in the last two decades. From the launching of the government's Community Development Project in 1969, official thinking has favoured the 'demonstration project'; such projects have figured in successive government initiatives – the inner area studies, Urban Programme funding and the like. The idea has been attractive because it gives the impression, at relatively low cost, that something is being done. Life for such projects is inevitably insecure, and their 'demonstrations' are in the event seldom taken up on a larger scale. So their birth and death rates are almost certainly higher than for indigenous local community groups.

In general, projects share many of the same characteristics as groups. The term is usually applied to a specific scheme for which funding is being sought. Such a project may fall under one of a number of headings – it may be an arts project (for a local arts festival or for community drama, music or dance), a community business project to provide work for local people and meet a local need, a project supporting community work to help particular kinds of disadvantaged people. Some community projects are broader in their functions, embracing a multi-purpose local community association carrying out a range of activities. Most community projects, whether single or multi-purpose, depend on the participation of community groups. Thus some, but by no means all, community groups are part of a community project and most community projects comprise one or more community groups. Many projects, like most groups, are set up by local residents, but projects and to a lesser extent groups are sometimes launched as a result of the efforts of 'intermediates' – external initiators including community workers.

Community projects and groups are obviously intended to help local people. Most set out to provide a service, to exert influence or both. Their relationship to the concept of community is clear: they see themselves as providing the service or exerting the influence on the part of all local people or of some people, whether local residents or not, who share a common interest, problem or need. Particularly when groups are set up as part of a community project or when community workers are employed, they have other aims as well, for example, to help people acquire new skills or develop community ties and attachment.

Most community groups are self-financing, but some of them – and many community projects – receive funds for staff or premises from charitable trusts, local authorities or central government (for example under the Urban Programme).

Community projects generally operate at a larger geographical scale than community groups. Community groups are mainly local, usually serving an area with a population of a few hundred. Sometimes, when they are serving a particular interest group, their area may be a borough, district or town, with a population of 50,000 or more. Self-help groups serving minorities may operate at a larger scale still – regional or even national.

Assessment
It is difficult to evaluate the contribution made by community groups to national life. In one sense community groups and projects are subject to a good deal of assessment at the local level. It is true that with many smaller groups – play groups, for example, or residents' associations – the issue is not raised; the local need is obvious, and people just want to get on with meeting it, without trying to measure the effectiveness of what they do. But many groups make some effort. Their founders and management committees want success and commonly see the need to gather information to demonstrate it. What is more, funding bodies such as local authorities, with an understandable need to be convinced that their money is being usefully applied, often require evidence about performance. Community projects funded by central government or local authorities – and groups created in the context of projects – are particularly likely to make attempts at evaluation.

But although all this fact-gathering goes on, there are many obstacles to systematic evaluation. Resources are seldom available for a carefully-designed study. There are often conflicts between project workers and researchers. The former are usually more concerned to get on with action, are suspicious of the researchers and may be too impatient – or too busy – to keep detailed records throughout the project's life. Again, the objectives and organisation are inevitably to some extent changed in the light of experience, and other circumstances change too, all of which makes it difficult to measure with any confidence exactly what has been achieved.

There have, however, been some useful studies. Hugh Butcher and his colleagues carried out 'comparative analyses' of six community groups in the north of England in the 1970s, three of them fruits of the government-funded Community Development Project[1]. They established an analytical framework to examine and compare the groups, and within this they assessed 'achievements, impact and failures'. An Action Committee on public transport was said to have 'made little headway'; its 'prospects for survival as a county and national pressure group... were bleak'. It was 'difficult to assess the impact' of a community association. Of a third group – a Joint Working Party on Vagrants – the researchers reported that the 'Short-term achievements...were substantial. Progress towards longer-term aims was less impressive'. A Senior Citizens Action Group was said to have been 'successful in achieving its self-organising and self-help objectives' but 'less successful in influencing the policy and practice of external organisations'. A local Action Group was judged generally successful, having had 'few failures in pursuing its objectives'.

As part of the European Community's Poverty Programme in the 1970s, seven 'family day centre' projects were established in Britain, six in the London area, one in Liverpool[2]. The projects were co-ordinated and monitored by Phyllis Willmott and Susan Mayne, who published an evaluation of them. The report concluded that 'substantial achievements were made by all seven of the family day centres', but it also pointed out some of the limitations and difficulties:

> Circumstances outside the project could – and did – change...
> Helping the very poor proved harder than helping those threatened
> with poverty... Inadequate or hasty preparation prevented the
> achievement of some objectives... [Some projects had] confused
> or over-ambitious aims.

A number of other studies have been published, several of them by the Community Projects Foundation. The reports of such studies mainly give a descriptive account of the life of the group or project, draw heavily on quotations from workers on the project, local councillors and officials, and sometimes include surveys of the local population. The studies show that few local people usually play an active part. A study of a street Residents' Housing Association in Edinburgh, for instance, reported:

> Nearly all of those interviewed had heard of [the project], although few were members or had any kind of involvement with the Association. Few felt that the Association had benefitted their household, although almost all said that it had benefitted others in the street[3].

A study by Marilyn Taylor of a community project in a 'British market town', where three residents' associations were established in the 1970s, concluded that there were 'practical improvements in living conditions' as a result, that the stigma from which one particular area had suffered was reduced and that participation in local activities increased. Though many local residents were members, only a minority were active:

> The formal membership of all three Asssociations was about 70 per cent of those eligible, but the active element in each was a much smaller Committee.

The 'most needy families – the materially and socially deprived' remained 'outside the sphere of the community groups'[4].

Another study by the same researcher, this time of a community project started in 1979 in a mining area in Warwickshire, reported that after two years:

> Group activity had increased markedly and had been sustained for the first time in living memory. At any one time during the life of the project there were usually 30 to 40 local people working actively with it. Over a period of two years about 200 people had been closely involved in this way, and a much wider number were in touch with the project...in a more limited way... Local people had acquired new skills... There had been concrete improvements in the general environment... [5].

A recent book describing a number of local projects concerned with promoting health included some assessments of their impact. One, a Way to Better Health Group set up by three women in

Nottingham, ran health education classes and relaxation classes. The report said that 'The fact that the group was started by some of the women who would be using it established an atmosphere of friendliness and sharing' and 'Quotations from participants testify that sessions were enjoyable and effective'. The conclusion drawn about a local campaign to improve health in an area of Tyne and Wear was:

> Gains made through (the) campaigns gave residents the confidence to tackle other longstanding issues: tangible results were that a doctor and community nurse were appointed to work with... educational sessions in youth clubs on sex education, relationships and puberty. A community midwife service has also been established... Through the project's community development approach, residents found ways of taking on more responsibility for, and control over, their health in the widest sense[6].

As suggested earlier, most of the systematic research on community groups has been of ones which were set up as part of community projects, usually with funding from official sources. In this sense, nearly all have been far from typical of community groups. A rare study, carried out by Barry Knight and Ruth Hayes in inner London, started with the community and tried to identify all the community groups in two small areas whose populations were about 8,000 and 5,000 respectively[7]. As the authors put it, 'we believe we tried every tactic available to uncover community activity'.

They found 12 groups in the larger area and six in the smaller. Of the total of 18 groups, eight were part of borough-wide organisations, seven were purely local and the remaining three operated at both levels. Figure 5 shows the variety. Most of the groups were interest communities as well as operating within an identifiable geographical area. The pensioners' association, black self-help group, under fives group and women's aid are clear examples. Of the remainder probably only the community arts group, community centre, residents' action group and tenants' and community association were general groups, in the sense of being intended to serve the needs of the general population of the locality.

The examples illustrate the point made earlier that community groups are created for a variety of immediate purposes, the main ones here being to combine for mutual aid (black self-help group, under fives group), to represent the interests of residents (residents' action group, tenants' and community association) and to provide a service or meet a particular need (drop-in for boys, befriending project).

Figure 5 Community groups identified in two London areas

Area A	Area B
community arts group	tenants' and community association
pensioners' association	catholic community association
community centre	visiting the elderly project
black self-help group	discussion club
drop-in for boys	youth action group
employment workshop	adventure playground
befriending project	
under fives group	
nursery	
play association	
women's aid	
residents' action group	

Source: Knight and Hayes (see reference 7)

The study was able to show which of the groups were indigenous and which were set up through the intervention of others. Two of the 18 groups had been formed by 'people...directly affected by the problem that the group was set up to solve', four by professional community workers employed by the local authority or voluntary bodies, four by clergymen and as many as eight by community activists (described by the researchers as 'typically...young, well-educated, middle class, and socially and politically committed').

In the absence of similarly comprehensive material from other places, it is impossible to say how far the number, types or origins of groups reflect more general patterns in inner areas or elsewhere. In contrast to virtually all the other studies of the kind referred to earlier, Knight and Hayes were rather critical of such groups, concluding: 'Community groups did little to create a feeling of community...did not reach the poorest...are marginal to inner city communities and do not effectively tackle their problems'. It has to be remembered, however, that this was only one study. It has not as yet been repeated elsewhere.

What makes for success?

David Donnison has carried out a review of 20 community-based projects in Britain and Ireland[8]. These included some based on single-purpose community groups, such as self-help groups 'offering mutual support to people who suffer from the same disease or handicap' but also 'broad-based community associations organising a wide range of activities'. The qualities that he suggested helped projects to succeed are shown in Figure 6.

Figure 6   Characteristics needed for community project success

Charismatic, committed leaders.
Key members with past experience of collective action, for example in a trade union, the Labour movement or a religious group.
Paid staff.
A flow of funds.
A building.
Friendly politicians or officials.
The capacity to establish a workable balance of power with local politicians.
Accountability to members, other local people and funders.
Financial accountability in particular.
Capacity to welcome newcomers and new ideas.

Source: Donnison (see reference 8)

Donnison's list – what he calls his 'ten commandments' – is a useful guide to those wanting to set up sizeable projects, or to keep ones going that already exist. Although some of the criteria are relevant to most other community groups as well, others are less so to certain types. All groups benefit from having committed leaders, preferably with some experience of running things, and from being open to new members and new ideas. All need to be accountable to funders, members and others they serve, and all need to organise their finances in a businesslike fashion. Key members with experience are always an advantage. But many of the smaller types of local group, for example those representing the tenants of a small housing estate or those running a fairly modest mother and toddler scheme on a mutual basis, can in the main manage successfully without paid staff, friendly politicians or officials, or a balance of power with local politicians. Although some community groups will benefit from having a building of their own, others will need no more than an occasional meeting room or may operate from members' homes.

Other guidance on community projects, as distinct from community groups, was given in the research report on family day centres mentioned earlier. The report's suggestions for running and assessing projects include these:

- *On methods* [There are] inherent risks of conflicts of interest (between users, between users and staff, between both and parent bodies or funders). Recognising such conflicts at an early stage is not an easy matter, and methods of resolving conflicts and implementing conciliatory action (so far as they exist) are not well developed.
- *On objectives* ... aims and objectives which are so broad as to make success or failure virtually impossible to measure should be avoided and... discouraged by funding bodies.
- *On evaluation* [It is important to have] clearly defined commitments and relevant structures between...projects, researchers and funders.

The general conclusion is that community groups and projects can be of clear value to their active members and to the other people they serve, but that there are a number of difficulties to which they are prone. These are at present not widely enough recognised. The more that is done to study such small-scale community initiatives, and the more the processes, the problems and the lessons from past experience are understood, the more successfully will they be able to play their part in public life.

References

1. H. Butcher, P. Collis, A. Glen and P. Sills, *Community Groups in Action: Case Studies and Analysis*, London, Routledge and Kegan Paul, 1980.
2. Phyllis Willmott and S. Mayne, *Families at the Centre: a Study of Seven Action Projects*, Occasional Papers on Social Administration No. 72, London, Bedford Square Press/National Council of Voluntary Organisations, 1983.
3. M. Dungate (editor), *Community Works 1: Aspects of Three Innovatory Projects*, London, Community Projects Foundation, 1980.

4. M. Taylor, A. Kestenbaum and B. Symons, *Principles and Practice of Community Work in a British Town*, Second Edition, London, Community Projects Foundation, 1983.
5. M. Taylor, *Inside a Community Project – Bedworth Heath*, London, Community Projects Foundation, 1983.
6. C. Chanan (editor), *Action for Health: Initiatives in Local Communities*, London/Edinburgh, Community Projects Foundation/Health Education Authority/Scottish Health Education Group, 1988.
7. B. Knight and R. Hayes, *Self-Help in the Inner City*, London, London Voluntary Service Council, 1981.
8. D. Donnison, 'Social policy and the community' in M. Bulmer, J. Lewis and D. Piachaud (editors), *The Goals of Social Policy*, London, Unwin Hyman, 1989.

6 Local Government Decentralisation

Despite the shift away from the centre represented by community policies, the present government is taking upon itself, in education, housing and financial arrangements, for example, some of the powers that formerly lay with local authorities. The recent trend in the relationship between central and local government has been to centralisation rather than its opposite. The decentralisation discussed in this chapter is within local authorities.

The current interest in local government decentralisation in Britain is, to some extent at least, a specific expression of public disenchantment with the 'reform' of local government in the 1960s and 1970s, when much larger authorities than previously existed were created on the basis of what is now seen to be inadequate evidence. British local government areas and populations are much larger and in consequence less accessible than anywhere else in the Western world. At least part of the logic guiding decentralising authorities is an attempt to reduce the effects of this within the existing structure.

The schemes initiated by local authorities in the 1980s need to be seen in the context of earlier decentralisation proposals. One type of scheme – for 'area management' – was encouraged by the Department of the Environment which funded experiments in six contracted local authority areas. Functions were delegated to the local level, the scale of 'local' varying from a population of 7,000 to one of 132,000; the main aims were to encourage co-ordination, develop 'community' involvement and improve the delivery of resources and services, particularly to deprived areas[1].

The other main approach has been to lay emphasis instead on representative local bodies, called 'neighbourhood councils' or 'community councils'[2]. The latter, proposed by the 1969 Royal Commission on Local Government in England and Wales[3], would in some respects have been similar to the community councils set up in Scotland and, on a different basis, in Wales.

Motives for decentralisation

Much of the recent impetus has come from Labour authorities, particularly left-wing ones. The pioneers were Walsall District Council and Sheffield City Council after the 1980 local elections. They were followed by several London boroughs after 1982, and later 'a growing number of major cities like Birmingham, Manchester, Edinburgh, Glasgow and Leeds as well as smaller towns like Basildon, Harlow and Reading'[4]. Decentralisation has also been undertaken by Liberal-controlled councils (for example, Tower Hamlets in London) and Conservative ones (for example, Cambridgeshire). A more limited decentralisation of social services, often in the form of a 'patch' style of community social work discussed later (in Chapter 9), has been carried out in Conservative East Sussex and Humberside, among others.

The objectives of current decentralisation schemes vary from authority to authority. Some left-wing Labour councillors have viewed it as a necessary return to their working-class roots, after what is seen as their betrayal and desertion by the governments of Wilson and Callaghan. Decentralisation is also often seen by the same people as providing a means of educating working-class electors into a greater class consciousness and a more participative role in the struggle against capitalism. Other councils are more concerned with decentralisation as a means to a better delivery of services, others to give their 'consumers' more say, others again to more effective management.

The range of motives have been reviewed by Paul Hoggett and Robin Hambleton[5]. Despite the diversity, councils are essentially interested in two main themes. They want to decentralise their services in order to make them more accessible to residents and thus ensure a prompter and more effective service. Alternatively (or, more typically, in addition) they want to devolve power to their electors – to move towards a more participatory style of local democracy.

Decentralising services
Local authorities have so far made more progress in decentralising services than in sharing power with electors. The main services decentralised are social services, housing allocation and management, rate and rent collection, building works (including council house repairs) and environmental health. Some authorities have also decentralised to the neighbourhood level the management of local planning, parks, libraries, refuse collection and street cleaning. Neighbourhood offices commonly house staff giving welfare advice as well as those dealing with services mentioned.

The process of decentralising services raises some problems[6]. One difficulty is staff objections. Staff are often resistant, partly because they fear redundancies or changes in their jobs, but sometimes because they think that professional standards may be lowered and a worse service provided.

Another problem is that decentralising may weakening specialised services. The argument for decentralisation, as for localised social work in particular, is that it can provide more effective support because the services are closer to local people and therefore more sensitive to their needs. The case against is that it may be incompatible with providing good specialised services to those who need them.

Sharing power
Though some difficulties arise with devolving services, the task is relatively straightforward compared with that of devolving power. For a start, local politicians often find it difficult to decide to do it, whatever they may have said in their manifestos. When it comes to the point, many councillors draw back. Another difficulty is that, as research has shown, local people are not particularly interested, at least if their role is presented in the way it usually has been. As John Gyford has put it, if the services are good people are unlikely to want to bother; if services are bad they may still baulk at giving up their Thursday evenings to go to meetings[7].

Apart from these doubts, decentralisation of power raises constitutional problems. If the process goes beyond a certain point, elected members and senior officers may not be able to ensure that their council's statutory responsibilites are met. Delegating power may also generate conflicts with council policy. How can a council devolve power to its citizens and at the same time ensure that a local committee does not take decisions contrary to the council's own priorities? Those priorities, reflecting the platform on which the council was elected, may legitimately be judged by councillors as in the interests of most of the authority's population as a whole, not just of those representing – or claiming to represent – those in a particular part of the authority's area.

There are also questions about the appropriate scale. The aim of sharing power with residents is usually envisaged as being implemented through a formal organisation at the neighbourhood level, whether neighbourhood forums as for example in the London borough of Islington or area committees as in Birmingham. But in practice the size of an authority's area and population, and of its decentralised districts or neighbourhoods, differ widely. This can be illustrated by the same two examples: Birmingham's areas contain populations of nearly 80,000 each, about 12 times greater than that of an average Islington neighbourhood. Which is the 'right' one?

It is, in any event, arguable that even an Islington neighbourhood is too remote from the lives of most local residents to generate much interest. People are much more likely to wish to participate, and be able to do so usefully, at a scale closer to their homes; they are also more likely to do so where the focus is upon something they can see is of direct concern to them.

For these reasons, what is sometimes called 'user control' – or would more accurately be described as 'user participation' – seems to work more effectively than a generalised decentralisation of power through neighbourhood councils or forums. Examples given by Gyford[8] are the involvement of tenants in managing their housing estate or parents their day nursery. The levels of decentralised operation, in those two instances, are the housing estate and the catchment area of the day nursery rather than a larger geographical neighbourhood.

Apart from such user involvement, there is also a strong case for local consultation and, where appropriate, negotiation when councils are preparing specific proposals affecting people's lives. Examples are a traffic management scheme and the building of a day nursery. If residents and other interested groups are consulted, the plans can take their views and concerns into account as far as possible. The discussions will often lead to a better solution than council officers and committees can devise on their own and, although the final decision will not necessarily please all of the various parties, they will

at least know more about the (usually complex) issues that needed to be resolved.

Fuller proposals in the context of decentralisation to involve people in decisions, not just about their estate or a specific local issue but about their neighbourhood more broadly, may be worth persevering with. The experiments will sometimes work with a high degree of success. How far they do so will depend on how the decentralisation is operated in practice. Sharing power with residents is more likely to make progress if for example the neighbourhoods are given budgets of their own, to spend as they choose on local matters. There is, alternatively, a case for reviving the idea of separate elected neighbourhood councils (urban parish councils), with specific budgets and distinct local powers, as proposed by the Association for Neighbourhood Councils[9].

Measures of success

There is little evidence to date showing how far decentralisation – of services or power – has had beneficial or deleterious results. Some evidence from Islington suggests that there have been measurable improvements. The speed of repair on council estates has increased, and backlogs in processing housing benefit were reduced. In social services, the demand for support went up, particularly in areas formerly distant from social services offices and, though there was no hard evidence about consumer satisfaction, the impressions were favourable[10]. A social survey in part of Islington in 1988 found high levels of satisfaction with the local neighbourhood centre and its work. For example 63 per cent of the sample said the neighbourhood office was 'successful' or 'very successful' for 'getting in contact with social services', and 58 per cent for 'giving people more say in how the council is run'[11].

Although such results are encouraging, it is difficult to be confident about what is and is not possible as a result of decentralisation measures, about the structures that work and those that are less successful, and under what conditions.

Interpretation is complicated by the fact that some of the forms of decentralisation that seem to work best, for example in housing, can be undertaken without the existence of a general framework of decentralised local government. This is true for example of refurbishment schemes on particular housing estates, where residents are involved in decisions, and where repair and other services are devolved to the estate level. It also applies to other forms of user control or participation, and to arrangements to consult local residents on particular issues. It is not clear, in other words, whether all or most of the aims of decentralisation could be achieved without a general formal structure of sub-councils or the like.

It is worth asking about the motives for local government decentralisation. It can be argued that decentralisation, certainly of housing services and perhaps more generally, is seen by some Labour local authorities as a means to counter the Conservative government's attacks on local government. This may have applied to housing in particular, as Ian Cole has suggested[12.] He argues that the reasoning was that, if it could be shown that council housing could be managed in a less bureaucratic and less centralised fashion, more responsive to tenants' needs and wishes, there would be less of a case for breaking up local authority housing empires and transferring the property to housing associations, housing trusts and the like. But, as Hambleton shows, this is certainly by no means the only motive. It seems likely that local politicians have, for the most part, genuinely believed that the process could give their customers better services and a more important role in local affairs.

Conclusion
Despite the doubts and problems, there clearly have been some achievements. The potential advantages of decentralising services and consulting local people are substantial, so long as these things are done well. But what does that mean? The lessons from the experience can be summed up as follows.

- Councils are right to concentrate at least in the first instance on decentralising services for more effective delivery rather than creating an authority-wide system to decentralise power to neighbourhoods. Sharing power with residents works best when it includes devolving resources and decisions, when it devolves power to a highly local level such as a housing estate, or when it means consulting residents about specific plans or proposals that will affect them directly.
- It is, however, by no means clear how far the accessibility, quality and speed of delivery of services depend on a formal structure of decentralised local government, and how far these results could be achieved by other means. In delivering social welfare, the devolution of resources to a case manager who is

working to provide a package of care for an individual client, seems at least as effective – probably more so – than devolution of the services to 'patches' or neighbourhoods. Some other successful forms of decentralisation, for example in schemes to upgrade local authority housing estates, apparently succeed by devolving management, repair and maintenance services and resident participation to the level of the estate rather than a larger neighbourhood.

• Decentralising authorities need to be explicit both about their precise objectives and about how they would measure success.

• Firmer evidence needs to be collected about performance against explicit objectives. One of the criticisms of the current round of decentralisation is that it has learnt nothing from the earlier experiments with area management, mini town halls and neighbourhood councils. In those earlier phases, as now, there was little serious effort to evaluate what was happening. Unless the experience this time is carefully monitored, we shall not know what works best, for what services and in what kinds of setting.

References

1. Department of the Environment, *Area Management Note*, London, Department of the Environment, 1974; for an interim assessment of these experiments, see C.J. Horn, T. Mason, K.M. Spencer, C.A. Vielba and B.A. Webster, *Area Management: Objectives and Structures*, Birmingham, Insitute of Local Government Studies, 1977.
2. Michael Young, 'A new voice for the neighbourhood', *What?*, 2 (2), 1970; Department of the Environment, *Neighbourhood Councils in England*, Consultation Paper, London, Department of the Environment, 1974.
3. Royal Commission on Local Government in England, *Report*, Vol. I, Cmnd 4040, London, HMSO, 1969.
4. R. Hambleton, 'Developments, objectives and criteria' in P. Willmott (editor), *Local Government Decentralisation and Community*, London, Policy Studies Institute, 1987, pp.8-24.
5. R. Hambleton and P. Hoggett, 'Beyond bureaucratic paternalism' in P. Hoggett and R. Hambleton (editors), *Decentralisation and Democracy: Localising Public Services*, Occasional Paper 28,

School for Advanced Urban Studies, University of Bristol, 1987, pp. 9-28.

6. See for example N.D. Deakin, 'Two cheers for decentralisation', in A. Wright, J. Stewart and N.D. Deakin, *Socialism and Decentralisation*, London, Fabian Society, 1984.
7. J. Gyford, 'Decentralisation and democracy' in P. Willmott (editor), op.cit., pp.58-64.
8. Ibid.
9. J. Perrin, *Democratically Elected Councils at Neighbourhood Level*, Birmingham, Association for Neighbourhood Councils, 1986.
10. L. du Parcq, 'Neigbourhood services: the Islington experience' in P. Willmott, op. cit., pp. 25-29.
11. P. Willmott, *Social Survey for Canonbury West Anti-Crime Initiative: Final Report to Islington Council*, London, Policy Studies Institute, 1989, p.21.
12. I. Cole, 'The delivery of housing services' in P. Willmott, op. cit., pp. 37-48.

7 Community Care

When, in 1957, the Royal Commission on the Law Relating to Mental Illness and Mental Deficiency recommended a shift from institutional care to community care it set in motion a far-reaching change in policy[1]. Accepted by all political parties, this policy has subsequently developed in two ways. First, the aim of community care has been extended to cover other sections of the population needing care as well as mentally ill and mentally handicapped people, including elderly people, people with physical handicaps and those suffering from chronic illness. Secondly, official policy has taken an ever broader view of the forms that care in the community takes. The range of support provided from public sources now includes not only the local authority domiciliary services and day centres proposed by the Royal Commission but also sheltered housing and special housing, hostels for mentally handicapped people, small local hospitals and homes, and respite care to relieve carers.

In addition to what is done by public services, community care includes private residential and domiciliary services (some of them largely subsidised out of public funds), the support given by voluntary organisations and self-help groups and the even more substantial informal care provided by relatives, neighbours and friends. The contribution of informal carers and local voluntary bodies was recognised in 1981, when the government, borrowing a distinction first made by Michael Bayley in 1973[2] between care in the community and care by the community, endorsed care by the community as the official objective[3].

Most of these developments were reflected in the Department of Health and Social Security's definition which formed part of its evidence, in 1984, to the House of Commons Select Committee on Social Services. The objectives of community care were described as:

- to enable the individual to remain in his own home wherever possible, rather than being cared for in a hospital or residential home;
- to give support and relief to informal carers (family, friends and neighbours) coping with the stress of caring for a dependent person;
- to deliver appropriate help, by the means which cause the least possible disruption to ordinary living;
- to relieve the stresses and strains contributing to or arising from physical or emotional disorder;
- to provide the most cost-effective package of services to meet the needs and wishes of those being helped;
- to integrate all the resources of a geographical area in order to support the individuals within it. The resources might include informal carers, NHS and personal social services and organised voluntary effort, but also sheltered housing, the local social security office, the church, local clubs, and so on[4].

Thus, as the concept is now understood, the essence of community care is that people needing care should as far as possible receive it in their own homes, and that they and their informal carers should be supported to facilitate this. If care at home is not possible, then small group homes or residential homes are seen as alternatives. This is a common 'community care' solution, for example, for people with mental handicaps who cannot easily live in their own homes.

The community in question, as the last paragraph of the DHSS statement suggests, is the geographical area surrounding the people being cared for. From the viewpoint of any service, however, the relevant geographical community is its local operational area or sub-area. Each service needs to identify a precise physical area with an appropriately-sized population within which it will work, rather than a potential attachment community, and the scale of these operational communities may well vary. In any event, most of the care that people receive comes from informal sources – from relatives, friends and neighbours. These networks of people do not constitute the local community in any meaningful sense of the term; the relatives and friends providing care and support may not even live locally. The notion of a recognisable geographical community within which the community care policy is operating locally has little correspondence with reality at present in most parts of the country.

Impact on people

The shift to community care has two dimensions – moving people out of the hospitals and institutions where they formerly lived, and keeping people out of such places who would formerly have gone into them. Some limited evidence is available about the effects of these policies in recent years. For example, the number of people in mental hospitals and units fell between 1971 and 1986 by over a third, while the number of patients attending outpatients clinics rose by about a fifth[5]. Such statistics, though useful, do not say anything about how the community care policy has been applied administratively or in terms of resources, or about how the people being cared for, or their informal carers, fare 'in the community'.

Community care policies constitute a sharper test of reality against aspiration than do most other community policies. A conscious decision was made to provide frail elderly, mentally handicapped, mentally ill and physically disabled people with a different style of care and in consequence a different – and better – pattern of daily life. To measure the achievement against the policy objectives should be a relatively clear-cut process, easier than with most other community initiatives. But there has been little systematic enquiry.

A review of studies of domiciliary care for elderly people showed that, compared with residential care, the benefits included higher morale, decreased loneliness, improved health, increased mobility, reduced dependence, increased social contact and increased capacity to cope[6]. A study of the housing and support available to 100 people discharged from London psychiatric hospitals found that as many as 86 of them preferred living outside hospital, and 93 said they were in regular contact with at least one professional worker (mainly day centre staff, psychiatrists, GPs, social workers and Community Psychiatric Nurses). On the other hand, 67 said they did not have an opportunity to discuss the housing options after discharge, as many as 80 were dissatisfied with their housing, 57 said they were dissatisfied with the support they were getting from statutory services, and 28 reported problems in managing their illness 'in the community'[7]. Another study, of 120 mothers in North Humberside with mentally handicapped children, reported that 'The mothers we talked to... received little help and many had to soldier on in relative isolation'[8].

The picture from small studies such as these, in different parts of the country and looking at different kinds of consumer of community care, is therefore mixed, part satisfaction and evidence of some support from community care services and part dissatisfaction and evidence of inadequacy.

The research on carers confirms that, although some help is given by neighbours and friends, the bulk of informal care comes from relatives, and that (apart from husbands caring for wives) the relatives are more often women than men, and are often daughters and daughters-in-law. The burdens are particularly heavy on some carers, including some of the parents of mentally or physically handicapped children, and some of those caring for dementing or physically frail elderly people. Again a mixed picture emerges, with a good deal of dissatisfaction with what many carers see as the limited support given by the formal health and social services.

Resources and administration
The administrative and financial arrangements have been the subject of a number of recent official enquiries, including those by the Audit Commission[9], the House of Commons Select Committee on the Social Services (which concentrated on community care for mentally handicapped and mentally ill people)[10], the National Audit Office[11] and Sir Roy Griffiths[12].

Most of the reviews report some successes. The Audit Commission, for example, cited encouraging examples of schemes supporting members of each of the main groups, and also a model local scheme providing 'caring for carers'. As the Commission commented, the examples 'demonstrate... that community-based care need not be just another attractive concept'.

But the most striking thing about the various reports is their consensus over the failings of community care. The Audit Commission said that it was 'in disarray', that 'progress has generally been slow, and in some places is not keeping up with the run-down of long-term institutions'. The National Audit Office confirmed that 'overall progress has been slower than the DHSS would have liked' and identified 'a wide range of difficulties'. The House of Commons Select Committee said that 'The stage has now been reached when the rhetoric of community care has to be matched by action'. Sir Roy Griffiths commented that 'Community care has been talked of for 30 years and in few areas can the gap between rhetoric and reality on the one hand, or between policy and reality in the field on the other hand have been so great'.

One of the difficulties is the organisational complexity. The implementation of community care depends on three central government departments (the Department of Health, covering social services and health, the Department of Social Security, covering social security and the Department of the Environment, covering housing and the funding of local authority social services). At the local level it involves the health authorities, social security offices, the family practitioner committees, the local authority social services departments, the local housing authorities, the local education authorities, the private sector, housing associations and a wide range of voluntary bodies and self-help groups, as well as millions of individual carers.

The effective delivery of services is not at all easy with such a complicated system. Apart from the complexity, formal agencies find it difficult enough to collaborate internally, because of historical rivalries and bureaucratice conservatism. It is even more difficult for them to cooperate with each other, and with the relatives, friends and neighbours who provide informal care[13].

Particular problems arise when one thrust of government policy works against another. An example is the separate funding of residential care through social security, described by the Audit Commission as generating 'perverse incentives' and by Sir Roy Griffiths as 'a particularly pernicious split in responsibilities, and a fundamental obstacle to the creation of a comprehensive local approach to community care'. The difficulties caused by this split were examined by a joint central and local government working party, which recommended that the assessment of need for residential care, the setting of standards for residential homes and the financing of care in them should all be placed with local authorities[14].

Residential care provides one example of a more general confusion of responsibilities, a point which Sir Roy identified as central:

> I emphasise responsibilities; collaboration, joint planning, joint finance are admirable provided that in the first place responsibilities are clear and, in the absence of collaboration, authorities can be held responsible.

The other main problem is resources. Some critics have suggested that the resources provided by the government have been inadequate, and that this applies in particular to the flow of funds to help ease the switch of people out of institutions into community care. Sir Roy Griffiths commented that it was not his 'remit to deal with the level of funding', but he noted that 'many of the local authorities and voluntary bodies grappling with the problems at local level certainly felt that the Israelites faced with the requirement to make bricks without straw had a comparatively routine and possible task'.

Discussion of the level of funding has always been difficult because the government does not set aside – indeed, no government has ever set aside – specific grants for community care. Hence the Griffiths recommendation that central government should contribute to local government 'a substantial proportion of the total public funds it estimates are needed to meet national objectives'. The government would in other words be obliged, for the first time, to say what it was prepared to pay for community care.

Two doubts

Apart from anxieties about the implementation of the policy in practice, two more basic doubts have been raised to community care as at present conceived.

The first was expressed in the review by the House of Commons Select Committee. It argued that, in effect, official policy had been too optimistic about how many mentally ill and mentally handicapped people could live successfully in the community: 'We must face the fact that some people need asylum'. The Committee said that, of course, the asylum must not be the kind of institution historically associated with that term.

To recognise that some patients are not suited to community care does not invalidate the general argument that it is to be preferred for – and is preferred by – most. Even the growth in private residential care, particularly for elderly people, does not undermine that general proposition, since though the proportions in private residential homes have grown they still account for only a small minority, if an increasing minority, of those receiving care.

The second fundamental question is about the burdens borne by carers, particularly women carers. Some feminists argue that the use of the term care *by* the community gives a misleading impression about the sources of such care. Their argument is that the care and the burdens – carried, as they emphasise, largely by unpaid women carers – constitute an exploitation of women; and that unless there is greater support for carers this exploitation will inevitably increase with any extension of informal care as an element in community care.

All this makes a convincing case for 'greater official support in the form of professionally-provided services and financial recompense'[15]. But some feminist critics go further and argue for 'an expansion of certain kinds of residential care' leading to 'a very different balance in the provision of care from the one which exists at the moment: much less from relatives, much more from collective resources, especially statutory provision'[16].

As suggested earlier, there needs to be choice – and that must apply to the carers as well as to those needing care. But if the formal services did their job better than they usually do at present, if they provided more adequate support for informal carers and if they meshed formal and informal care more successfully, the carers' task would become less onerous than it sometimes is now. The case for the critics' proposal to switch towards formal services – and away from informal care in people's own homes – would then be less strong. All in all, making community care work more effectively in such ways seems to remain the best option.

Conclusions

Of all the community initiatives, the official policy of community care is perhaps the one with the biggest potential impact on people's lives. It epitomises what I described in Chapter 4 as a common theme – the movement away from large impersonal structures to decentralised arrangements which, at their best, work closely with what people want, with what they do for themselves and with what members of informal social networks do for each other.

Despite the failings of community care as currently organised and financed, most agencies and most people remain in favour of the idea; as the House of Commons Select Committee put it: 'None of those who submitted evidence to us were opposed to the basic principles of community care'.

There are plenty of reasons for welcoming the policy, as long as it can be made to work properly. The main thrust remains sound: in its rejection of large and bureaucratic institutions; in its recognition of the desire of most people to live in their own homes if possible or, if not, in a familiar and 'normal' environment; in its recognition that most people needing social care already do live like that and are able to do so because of the support and care provided by relatives and others; in its objective of meshing together such informal support with the domiciliary, day and respite care that can be provided by official and voluntary services. People themselves should choose the kind of care they want, but all the evidence is that most of the time most of those needing care favour the community-based version.

Community care also provides the clearest example of the gap between promise and performance. The various official reports indicate what is wrong and, though there is room for disagreement about details, about the kinds of things that need to be done. If the main criticisms are accepted by the government, and a sensible set of reforms implemented, then community care will become a reality over the next five or ten years. If not, the disenchantment will be even greater than it is now.

References

1. Royal Commission on the Law Relating to Mental Illness and Mental Deficiency 1954-57, *Report*, Cmnd. 169, London, HMSO, 1957.
2. M.J. Bayley, *Mental Handicap and Community Care*, London, Routledge and Kegan Paul, 1973.
3. Department of Health and Social Security (also Scottish Office, Welsh Office and Northern Ireland Office), *Growing Older*, Cmnd 8173, London, HMSO, 1980.
4. House of Commons Select Committee on the Social Services, *Community Care With Special Reference to Adult Mentally Ill and Mentally Handicapped People*, London, HMSO, 1985, pp. 5-6.
5. Central Statistical Office, *Social Trends 18*, London, HMSO, 1988, p. 126.
6. A. Salvage, *Developments in Domiciliary Care for the Elderly*, London, King's Fund, 1984.
7. A. Kay and C. Legg, *Discharged to the Community: a Review of Housing and Support in London for People Leaving Psychiatric Care*, London, Housing Research Group, City University, 1986.
8. S. Ayer and A. Aleszewski, *Community Care and the Mentally Handicapped: Services for Mothers and their Mentally Handicapped Children*, London, Croom Helm, 1984.
9. Audit Commission for Local Authorities in England and Wales, *Making a Reality of Community Care*, London, HMSO, 1986.

10. House of Commons Select Committee on the Social Services, op. cit.

11. National Audit Office, *Community Care Developments*, Report by the Comptroller and Auditor General, London, HMSO, 1987.

12. Griffiths Report, *Community Care: Agenda for Action*, A Report to the Secretary of State for Social Services by Sir Roy Griffiths, London, HMSO, 1988.

13. See for example P. Willmott, *Social Networks, Informal Care and Public Policy*, London, Policy Studies Institute, 1986, pp.105-119.

14. Firth Report, *Public Support for Residential Care*, Report of a Joint Central and Local Government Working Party, London, DHSS, 1987.

15. G. Dalley, Review of P. Willmott (see note 14), *Radical Community Medicine*, Summer, 1987, pp. 48-49.

16. J. Finch, 'Community care and the invisible welfare state', *Radical Community Medicine*, Summer 1986, pp. 15-22.

8 Community Policing

What distinguishes community policing from other policing is that the police introduce deliberate measures to promote closer collaboration with the community. The first aim is to build and maintain a partnership between the police and local people in preventing and combating crime. A second and related aim is to make the police more accountable to the public in their area.

Community policing takes a variety of forms.

- *More beat policemen* Variously described as 'home beat officers', 'resident beat officers', 'area beat officers', 'neighbourhood beat officers' and 'community constables', these are intended to be – as police officers are thought to have been in the past – familiar local figures, in close touch with local residents and shopkeepers, and therefore aware of what is going on. Above all, they are expected to work cooperatively with local people and mesh their own police work with the informal policing – or 'informal social control' – that members of the community themselves exercise over potential criminals and delinquents.
- *Neighbourhood watch* Sometimes called community watch, home watch or (with blocks of flats) tower watch. Working with the police, people in a small area come together to provide mutual surveillance. Neighbourhood watch is encouraged and supported by the police as a localised method of combining informal social control and police-community collaboration.
- *Crime prevention schemes* Since the mid-1960s crime prevention has been encouraged at the local level by crime prevention panels, composed of local representatives along with the police. At least initially the panels mostly concentrated on

working with business and industry. But a circular from the Home Office and four other government departments in 1984 tried to broaden the basis. It said 'effective crime prevention needs the active support of the community...police effectiveness cannot be greatly increased unless the community can be persuaded to do more for itself'[1]. A number of local crime prevention schemes have been established to promote this.

- *Collaboration with other agencies* The 1984 circular also said 'crime prevention schemes are more successful where the police and local agencies work together in a co-ordinated way towards particular aims'. Inter-agency collaboration had been proposed, and tried out in some areas, before then. The idea is that liaison between the police and other local services will again help to reduce crime. The relevant council agencies include those dealing with housing management, social services, architecture and planning; local voluntary organisations and residents' groups are often included as well. Education is seen as particularly important, with the police visiting local schools and establishing good relationships with children.

- *Police-community consultative committees* These are intended to provide a means by which representatives of the community cooperate with – and can influence the policies of – the police. Under Section 106 of the Police and Criminal Evidence Act, 1984, arrangements have to be made in each police area in England and Wales to obtain 'the views of people' in the area about policing of their area and 'their cooperation with the police in preventing crime'.

- *Lay visitors to police stations* This scheme, first recommended by the House of Commons Committee for Home Affairs and later endorsed by the Scarman Report on Brixton, involves random checks by members of panels of lay visitors on how local police interrogate and detain suspects.

Extent and geographical scale
All these measures have been, or are being, introduced in at least some places, but the extent of operation varies from scheme to scheme and from one police authority to another. Also the size of the area covered differs as between the different schemes.

Virtually every police force in the country now has some beat policemen. The area covered by a beat police officer varies, from about half a square mile in densely populated urban areas to many square miles in suburban or rural areas.

At the end of 1988 there were 64,000 neighbourhood watch schemes in England and Wales involving three and a quarter million households. The area of a watch scheme is usually about the size covered by a residents' or tenants' association, typically including a hundred or so households.

Crime prevention panels have been set up in every police force area. They usually operate at the level of a police subdivision, with a population of between about 40,000 and 150,000. There is no systematic information about how many local crime prevention schemes there are nor about the extent to which arrangements for inter-agency cooperation, whether directly linked to crime prevention panels or independent of them, thave been set up in local areas. Such cooperation can take place at different geographical levels from a housing estate to a police subdivision.

Following the 1984 Police and Criminal Evidence Act, Home Office circulars proposed the creation of consultative committees. Although they are not always called that, such committes have now been established by every police force in England and Wales. They are encouraged to link up with, or even merge with, crime prevention panels, though the extent to which and ways in which this has been done are not known. Consultative committees operate at a borough level in London, and normally at the level of a police subdivision elsewhere in the country.

Lay visitors' schemes, after being tried between 1983 and 1985 in six selected areas, were 'commended' to police forces in a Home Office circular in 1986, and now operate in most forces, either on a comprehensive basis or for inner urban areas. The areas covered by the schemes are the same as those for consultative committees – police subdivisions outside London, boroughs inside London. Outside London, the visitors are usually also members of police authorities, consultative committees or both; in London, where there is no elected policy authority, visitors are commonly members of consultative committees.

Evidence of success?
Some studies have tried to evaluate the effectiveness of different elements of community policing. They have pointed to some successes. At the same time, they have shown not only some of the problems with the various schemes, but also some of the difficulties of assessment.

Critics say that one problem with beat policing, for example, is that there is ambiguity over what beat officers are supposed to do; they lack a clear job description. Another difficulty is that, although on the basis of surveys it can be rightly argued that most people want more foot patrols, the same surveys show that they also want a rapid response when they dial 999. Without greater resources being devoted to policing they cannot have more of both[2].

Beat officers account for only a small proportion of manpower in most forces, typically about 5 per cent, rising to 15 per cent in a force like Hampshire where there has been a deliberate effort to transfer officers[3]. Even the officers who are supposedly permanently on the beat spend little time there in practice. A Home Office study in 1981-82 showed that on average the community involvement work carried out by such officers amounted to five hours a week. As David J. Smith has put it: 'there was no indication that permanent beat officers were, in general, engaging with the community to any significant extent'[4].

There has been little research on the impact on crime of any increase in beat policing. Such studies as have been done suggest that its introduction does not lead to much increased contact between police officers and members of the public. One result is more reported crime, but at the same time there is little sign of any reduction in actual crime or in people's fears of it[5].

The only study so far carried out of the relationship between the informal policing carried out by residents and local business people and that carried out by the police is broadly in line with these findings[6]. It showed that the police view of their task was usually different from that of local people. In any event police officers themselves varied in their perspectives depending on their position within their forces. In general the characteristic police response did not blend at all easily with what people themselves did by way of policing. Indeed, in the words of the researchers, formal policing can 'easily undermine informal policing by the public'.

There have been a number of assessments of neighbourhood watch schemes but the picture emerging from the research is confused. In May 1988 John Patten, the Home Office Minister responsible for crime prevention, noted that residential burglaries had fallen by 5 per cent from 1986 to 1987, while the number of neighbourhood watch schemes had increased, implying that the one had caused the other[7]. Other Ministers and some Chief Constables had earlier reported reductions in crime following the introduction of neighbourhood watch.

A postal survey of 165 neighbourhood watch schemes carried out by Sohail Husain, a researcher from Southampton University, also seemed to produce encouraging results. The survey showed large proportions of respondents reporting success: 71 per cent said the schemes were 'successful' or 'very successful' in 'preventing crime', and the comparable proportions were 92 per cent with 'providing a sense of security', 73 per cent with 'improving police-public relations' and 65 per cent with 'improving community spirit'[8].

But a study by Trevor Bennett, a Cambridge University criminologist, produced less favourable conclusions. Bennett's study compared what happened in two neighbourhood watch schemes in London (in Acton and Wimbledon) with what happened in two comparable London areas. The research showed that reporting rates and clear-up rates hardly changed in the two neighbourhood watch areas, while the extent of recorded crime actually increased. There were, however, some positive gains; in the Acton neighbourhood watch area people became less anxious about crime against property over the period of the study and their sense of 'social cohesion' increased[9].

It is difficult to interpret these apparently conflicting findings. Most of the favourable results seem to be based on limited research. The Husain study in particular, though carefully executed, suffered from two weaknesses. Only just over half of the neighbourhood watch schemes approached took part in the survey, suggesting that perhaps those which did were the keenest and most successful ones; and, as Husain pointed out, the postal questionnaires were completed by 'the scheme co-ordinators who might be expected to have a positive bias towards neighbourhood watch which coloured their response'. The Bennett study, with its negative conclusions, was the most rigorous examination of neighbourhood watch so far undertaken.

John Patten, speaking for the Home Office, said of the Bennett study that it 'confirmed our view that the effectiveness of a neighbourhood watch scheme depends greatly on the quality of its organisation, and the degree of commitment which it is able to obtain from local people'. He added that 'neighbourhood watch is comparatively new to this country and there are still lessons to be learned'. To sum up, it looks as if under certain conditions neighbourhood watch may help reduce crime, but the evidence is far from conclusive. More thought is needed, not only about how neighbourhood watch can best be implemented and supported, but also about its basic assumptions.

It is a rather similar story with crime prevention and multi-agency collaboration (local agencies including such council services as housing management, education, planning and personal social services departments working closely with the police). Mollie Weatheritt says that crime prevention schemes in local areas seem to have had little success[10]. An evaluation by the Home Office Research and Planning Unit[11] of a demonstration project on inter-agency cooperation in Greater Manchester to reduce school burglaries concluded that the initiative was not a success, largely because of problems of implementation. The multi-agency approach itself was the main reason for failure; 'because a number of agencies were involved, none of them had sole or prime responsibility, and none had to give the matter the highest priority'[12].

Alice Sampson and her colleagues, reviewing a number of multi-agency schemes in inner city areas, concluded that 'the multi-agency approach should not be uncritically considered as offering a panacea for the plight of the inner cities... Multi-agency initiatives can and do fail; and unintended and unfortunate consequences often occur because initiatives are based on over-simplified assumptions'. Among other problems, the researchers referred to the 'structural conflicts between the state agencies' and 'tensions within localities'[13].

The most thorough research so far on police-community consultative committees is by Rod Morgan[14]. His analysis suggests that, although such committees can be of value in ventilating local problems and promoting cooperation, they have at least so far not had much success in building the hoped-for partnership between the police and the community. Morgan suggests various explanations for this failure: 'confusion and ignorance' about their responsibilities on the part of committee members, the lack of education to help them in their role, the negative response to the police and the committees – for understandable reasons – from certain elements in the community, the reluctance of the police forces – for equally understandable reasons – to provide adequate information to the committees or to treat them as much more than public relations forum. A particular problem, as Morgan points out, is that the areas covered by the committees are too large for them to connect with the community at the local scale.

Little is yet known about the effectiveness of lay visitors' schemes, which are however currently being assessed on a national basis, again by Rod Morgan, with Home Office funding. He pointed out in an initial statement that 'Lay visiting to police stations raises many complex and sensitive questions (access, confidentiality, procedures when complaints are received or deficiencies found)'[15].

Thus the available evidence over the range of community policing measures encourages scepticism rather than optimism about the extent to which they succeed in meeting their objectives. David J. Smith has argued that the apparent poor progress of community policing so far results not merely from the inevitable time lag, from the lack of experience or from the technical problems of implementation but from more fundamental dilemmas[16].

Smith gives three examples. First, most of the functions of the police are 'adversarial' and can therefore only with difficulty be reconciled with the notion of consensus. Second, it is difficult to establish the essential goodwill of the community towards the police because in many localities the police have to deal not with one community but with several and almost inevitably have easier relationships with some (elderly, white) than with others (young, black). Third, there are basic conflicts between the rule of law and two key features of community policing – decentralisation and 'flexibility' of treatment; the police cannot hold fast to the principle of equal treatment before the law and at the same time to a substantial extent make on the spot decisions in responding 'sensitively' (that is, differentially) to the same behaviour by different people.

This last conflict was recognised by Her Majesty's Chief Inspector of Constabulary in his 1985 report when he said that, although senior police officers remained commited to community policing, they also recognised that '...the need for police officers to understand and be responsive to the communities they serve must not undermine the firm and even-handed enforcement of the law and the effective control of disorder'[17].

Dilemmas like these perhaps underlie the very attractiveness of the community policing idea for many senior police officers, civil servants and politicians. The police today are under immense pressure – much greater than in the past. They are caught in a series of conflicting demands. They are expected somehow to reconcile differences within the community and differences between the police and some community elements whose members may be hostile. In a climate of growing sensitivity to minority interests and ever present fear that confrontation may lead to violence, the police are expected both to keep the peace and to avoid provocation. Community policing may seem attractive to them and to policy-makers because it seems to offer some solution to these almost irreconcilable tensions.

If all this is accepted – the new and fundamental dilemmas facing the police, the vagueness of the notion that community policing offers a solution, and the evidence to date of little progress – the right conclusion might well seem to be that community policing represents little more than a public relations exercise, rather than a genuine change in policing methods. Many of those concerned with policing policy, including senior police officers, would naturally dispute that. They would argue that it is difficult to make such fundamental changes in practice, that it is too early to make comprehensive judgements on the basis of fairly limited innovations evaluated over relatively short periods, and that early successes should not be expected, since the police force is engaged on a long-term investment in the minds of its young officers. As Her Majesty's Chief Inspector of Constabulary said in his 1984 report:

> It is always difficult to assess the effectiveness of community policing schemes since many of their benefits will only emerge in the long term[18].

Conclusion
Where does the balance of truth lie? The entirely cynical view should surely be rejected. Few people would disagree with the objectives of community policing, and in present conditions there is really no alternative to a community-based approach, difficult though it may be to give substance to it in practice. But progress will continue to be slow, or may never be achieved, unless politicians, the Home Office,

the police service and members of the public accept the following points.

- Police forces, with the help of the Home Office, need to be more explicit – to themselves and to others – about the precise aims of the different elements of community policing, and about how it is hoped to achieve them.
- Police forces need to say explicitly how they would measure success, and there needs to be a systematic and rigorous evaluation of what happens in the different applications of community policing in at least a sample of forces.
- The deep-seated conflicts of interest between different sets of people in a locality, and sometimes between certain sets of people and the police, have to be recognised. There needs to be some machinery which can make it possible for negotiation to take place where necessary over policing matters between the different interests themselves and between them and the police.
- Formal structures for collaboration between the police and the community are at present too remote from people's own experience. For most local community purposes, the police subdivision is 'the stratosphere', in Rod Morgan's term, and even local beat areas are too large[19]. There need to be police-public forums at a smaller geographical scale than the consultative committees.
- At a larger scale the existing police authorities need to be replaced by new and more effective arrangements through which representatives of the public can influence policing policy and practice at the force level. There are some politically entrenched attitudes on this subject, and the whole matter requires examination by an independent committee of enquiry.
- Whatever the future arrangements at the force level, they will not work unless the authorities representing the public have enough staff of their own, enough resources to collect information for themselves about police performance and appropriate training for their members and how to do their job. The same applies to local consultative committees. At all levels a genuine partnership between the police and the community they serve depends on official recognition, backed by resources, of the need to train and support community representatives.

A possible criticism of suggestions like these is that they would require resources. But it can be reasonably argued that a better strategy for police-community cooperation, and the more effective crime prevention that would be likely to result, would pay dividends. As Jon Bright has argued, a broader approach to crime prevention could be more cost-effective:

> Crime itself imposes an increasingly heavy burden on society through public expenditure on the criminal justice system (£4,800 million on prisons, police, courts and probation service in 1986/87) as well as the costs to local authorities and the victims themselves. A broad-based, well thought out, preventive strategy is not only likely to be more effective but makes good financial sense as well[20].

References
1. Home Office Circular 8/1984, *Crime Prevention*, p. 2.
2. See for example T. Jones, B. Maclean and J. Young, *The Islington Crime Survey: Crime, Victimisation and Policing in Inner London*, Aldershot, Gower, 1986, p. 115.
3. D.J. Smith, 'The police and the idea of community', in P. Willmott (editor), *Policing and the Community*, London, Policy Studies Institute, 1987, p.59.
4. Ibid., p.59.
5. D.J.Smith, op.cit., p. 60 and M. Weatheritt, *Innovations in Policing*, London, Croom Helm, 1985.
6. J. Shapland and J. Vagg 'Policing by the police and policing by the public' in P. Willmott (editor), op.cit., pp. 21-28.
7. *Hansard*, 13 May 1988, cols. 256-258.
8. S. Husain, *Neighbourhood Watch in England and Wales: a Locational Analysis*, London, Home Office, Crime Prevention Unit Paper 12, 1988.
9. T. Bennett, *An Evaluation of Two Neighbourhood Watch Schemes in London*, Cambridge, University of Cambridge Institute of Criminology, 1987.
10. M. Weatheritt, 1985, op.cit.
11. T. Hope, *Implementing Crime Prevention Measures*, Home Office Research and Planning Unit, Research Study 86, London, HMSO, 1985.
12. D.J. Smith, op.cit., p.60.

13. A. Sampson, P. Stubbs, D. Smith, G. Pearson and H. Blagg, 'Crime, localities and the multi-agency approach', *British Journal of Criminology*, forthcoming.
14. R. Morgan, 'The local determinants of policing policy' in P. Willmott (editor), op.cit., pp. 29-44.
15. R. Morgan assisted by C. Maggs, *Setting the P.A.C.E.: Police Community Consultation Arrangements in England and Wales*, Bath, University of Bath, Bath Social Policy Papers 4, 1985.
16. D.J. Smith, op.cit., pp. 54-67.
17. Her Majesty's Chief Inspector of Constabulary, *Report for the Year 1985*, House of Commons Paper 437, London, HMSO, 1986, p.50.
18. Her Majesty's Chief Inspector of Constabulary, *Report for the Year 1984*, House of Commons Paper 469, London, HMSO, 1985, p.50.
19. R. Morgan, op.cit., p. 42 and J. Shapland and J. Vagg, op.cit., pp.22-23.
20. J. Bright, 'Community safety, the community and the police', in P. Willmott (editor), op.cit., pp. 45-53.

9 Community Architecture

Community architecture, as the authors of a recent book on the subject explain, is 'based on the simple principle that the built environment works better if the people who use it are directly and actively involved in its creation and management'[1]. The suggestion that tenants should participate in the design of their homes was made in the report of a study of new housing schemes in 1953[2], and in the 1950s and 1960s some architects designing public housing were already using surveys of tenants to draw upon their wishes and experience[3]. But the historians of community architecture date its beginnings from 1967, when the Shelter Neighbourhood Action Project (SNAP) in Liverpool installed a resident architect to work with a community group, and 1968, when another architect set up his office in Byker, Newcastle to involve slum dwellers in designing their new council homes[4].

The Royal Institute of British Architects (RIBA) has described community architecture as 'the involvement of the public in the design of the built environment', and has drawn attention to a key difference in the relationship with the client compared with that in traditional architecture. Clients have of course always been consulted; the current concept is of two clients, a 'funding client' and a 'user client', the second being consulted at least as fully as the first[5].

The advocates of community architecture argue that if users are involved in the design of buildings – their homes and, for that matter, other kinds of building as well – the outcome is likely to be better than it otherwise would be. The buildings will be more suited to their purposes. They also suggest that the occupants are likely to do more to look after an environment they have helped to fashion than one designed for them by someone else, however well-meaning.

The alternative label 'community technical aid' is sometimes used for an approach which has much in common with the one so far described. This second movement grew up because some other professionals concerned with the environment – for example, surveyors, town planners and landscape architects – argued that what was known as community architecture was not just 'architecture' but was, and should be, more broadly based. They also argued that local people should be involved and consulted over wider planning issues affecting their lives, as well as the buildings, and the Town and Country Planning Association, which shares this view, has been associated with this approach.

A number of local community technical aid centres, providing a range of advice and help to groups of local residents, have been established and these are linked through a national body, the National Association of Community Technical Aid Centres. Thus there are two strands within the general movement towards fuller participation by users in shaping their environment, the one broader in the range of participating professionals and in its local geographical scale than the other. I use the term 'community architecture' to cover both.

Assessment

So many mistakes were made in the post-war years by architects designing public housing without consulting tenants that it must make for a better result if more notice is taken of residents. If professionals, and particularly architects, actually talk to – and listen to – the people who are going to have to live in the homes they rehabilitate or build, this must lead to greater sensitivity and sounder design.

It is not easy to go beyond these general conclusions, because there is so little to go on. In arguing their case, community architects offer evidence which, though largely impressionistic and anecdotal, shows that what they do is appreciated by at least some tenants and almost certainly has beneficial effects. Two architects working on a London scheme cite, for example, a letter they received from 26 tenants:

> Many thanks to you both, from us the tenants of Newquay House. You have opened up a new life to us with your kindness and consideration, knitted together a community that was straying apart, shown us there was hope in a decaying area and worked and fought very hard, long hours... Not only are you our architects, you have become our friends[6].

Some individual tenants in another scheme – the refurbishment of a local authority 'sink' estate in Hackney, London – were also enthusiastic:

> It's been absolutely wonderful. We've been involved in everything that's happened here from the very beginning. We've made decisions that no other council tenants have ever made.
>
> Through participating, we helped to become a community, to get people to live together, to work together, to communicate together. I hope the experience on these flats will happen on other estates, that other people will get the sort of involvement that we were lucky enough to get, so that they will get the homes they want rather than the homes they are just given[7].

There is also some statistical evidence about the same estate, suggesting that after the renovation of the estate 'crime and vandalism were virtually eliminated, common areas remained spotless, people's health – both physical and psychological – improved dramatically...' and that the comparison with a nearby estate, renovated without tenant involvement, is stark: within six months the other estate 'had reverted to a slum... the estate is still vandalised, ground floor flats are boarded up, tenant morale is low[8].

Other research shows, however, that community architecture is not without its problems. One study examined three schemes, all as it happens new brick-built terraces of housing on small sites. Using the Department of the Environment's Housing Appraisal Kit, this compared residents' satisfactions on these three schemes with those on 42 conventionally designed housing estates. Tenants' satisfaction was in some respects somewhat higher on the community architecture estates, and on one of them in particular, but the differences were not large. The conclusion drawn was that part of the explanation was that, like conventional schemes, community architecture had to operate within the same financial and administrative constraints. The scope for community architecture to influence the outcome is limited because it cannot add to the resources available or avoid the ultimate control of external organisations[9].

Participation was examined in the same study. It found that the professionals were commonly mistrusted by tenants. In general, relationships with tenants were stressful and plagued with difficulties. A local government officer who recorded the case history of a council community architecture project reported other problems. She found, not surprisingly, that in her local authority scheme there were strong pressures from different elements within the council, and that tenants disagreed with each other and with their representatives[10].

I examined another scheme myself. The task was to modernise a small estate of flats in the heart of the West End, previously owned by a charitable trust, then acquired by the Greater London Council and now transferred to a housing association. As well as having a series of discussions with the architects and interviewing officers of the housing association, I went as an observer to some of the regular meetings with tenants' representatives and I received reports on all. The meetings were primarily with a panel of representatives from different parts of the estate but were open to any tenants who wished to attend. Over the initial year of the project the meetings were mainly held fortnightly with some longer gaps of three or four weeks.

The estate contained over 150 flats and therefore at least 150 people could have attended. In practice the numbers were, not surprisingly, much smaller. The largest attendance was at an initial public meeting, to which 53 tenants went. Thereafter the highest number was 31, eight of them representatives and 23 other tenants, and the lowest numbers of attenders were seven, three and four respectively.

The meetings followed a standard pattern. On the initial discussion of the record of the previous meeting, some people with particular interests would seek to reopen debate on them and some who had not attended would object both to the views attributed to tenants generally and to the decisions taken. After these difficulties had been more or less resolved, the architects would introduce a new topic, such as the use of the open spaces between blocks, the design of windows or the plans for kitchens. They would explain that they were offering options. There would then be a long and often fierce discussion, sometimes based on a misunderstanding of the architects' intentions or a failure to recognise the constraints within which the architects had to work. Sometimes there were open conflicts between different groups of tenants, for instance between those who favoured new amenities and those who wanted to keep the rents down.

The atmosphere would then cool, as the architects or some of the tenants themselves would clarify the issues or move towards other peoples' positions. By the end of the meeting some sort of broad consensus had usually emerged. The result was that each time the architects either ended up with a decision in favour of one of the suggested options or promised to think again about an alternative.

Often the points at issue would be relatively small ones, like the choice of windows or kitchens just mentioned. Sometimes they would be more fundamental. An example was an early discussion about the future population of the estate and the dwellings needed for it. The architects raised two points. First they said that, projecting the present population into the future, the estate could be expected to contain more very elderly people and the scheme should perhaps include sheltered housing for them, with a resident warden. Secondly they suggested that perhaps, as a matter of policy, families with young children might be encouraged to live on the estate, with new dwellings being created for them. On both these issues the architects said their minds were open, but they presented the suggestions as if they were to some extent committed.

Most tenants present attacked both ideas. Those who spoke argued that the plans would turn parts of the estate into 'ghettos'; the forecasts about the numbers of very elderly people were wrong because in practice dependent elderly people would not wish to stay on; the estate and the vicinity could never provide a decent environment for families with young children and it would be unwise to plan for more than the few such families who, as now, felt they needed to live on the estate to be near their work. These views may have concealed a defence of what they saw as their own interests – perhaps they did not want their lives disturbed by increases in the numbers of dependent elderly people or noisy children among their neighbours. But in this case, as in many others, what they said seemed reasonable enough; after a heated debate the proposals on elderly people were modified and only a small number of family flats were provided.

Thus the process was lengthy and at times frustrating for both parties. The tenants often thought that the architects' purpose was just to pretend to consult as a concession to the current fashion and to tenant demands; that the architects had come with preconceived views, or with orders from the (equally distrusted) housing association landlords. In another community architecture scheme in central London which I looked at more briefly, the experience was much the same. The architects reported conflicts between tenants and more general difficulties between architects and tenants.

Both the London teams of architects were conscious of the low attendance at meetings. Both tried hard to contact residents by other means in seeking their views. The complementary methods used included a regular newsletter to all tenants, open days including evenings and weekends, and surveys to collect information about tenants' circumstances and views or to test their opinions on specific topics. Such methods succeeded in reaching more people, and were valued by the architects as useful additional tools. They were appreciated by at least some of the tenants who could not easily attend meetings.

Conclusions

I suggested in the previous chapter that perhaps Home Office officials and senior police officers, recognising the new problems that police forces faced in their relationships with the public and particularly with members of minority communities, saw community policing as helping the police to find a way out of their difficulties. At the same time, as I argued in the same chapter, neither the Home Office nor the police seem to have thought clearly enough about what they are doing.

It seems to me that much the same applies to community architecture. Following the high rise and other mass housing disasters of the 1950s and 1960s, it looked as if the brave new world had turned to dross. The high hopes of post-war reconstruction seemed to have been betrayed, and betrayed, what is more, by architects and town planners, the two professions which had seemed to offer so much. The reputation of the architectural profession plummeted, its public esteem was low. What could be more natural than that some of the the younger architects just qualifying should look for a new ideological base, an alternative to Le Corbusier, high rise and mass housing, and found it in a new approach that took architecture back to the people.

Some suggestions can be offered for the future.

- Architects and their supporters should not claim too much for the community approach. Housing depends on resources, and community architecture is unlikely to add to these. Nor can the approach revitalise the inner city, though it can do something to raise morale – a necessary condition for revival.
- One lesson from past projects is that, because only a minority of residents will attend meetings, no one chain of communication with tenants will suffice. A plurality of complementary methods, including sample surveys, is needed as well.
- It is also important to be clear about the circumstances in which community architecture is not appropriate and other methods

need to be used instead. It is not usually possible to consult tenants for new-build schemes, and in those cases in particular it is important to use sample surveys of tenants similar to those to be rehoused, in order to find out not only their views about their present homes and estates but also how they use the dwellings and environments.

• So far community architecture is conceived as a one-off process for each project, a means of involving tenants in design. There is an absence of general thinking about the lessons. Architects should be able to begin to draw conclusions about the kinds of design that are likely to work best for different sorts of resident; this would be particularly helpful for new-build schemes, where the tenants may not yet have been identified.

• Community architecture should also be able to offer some contribution to the wider debate about how public and other forms of social housing should be developed and managed, or indeed about what, in general, the relationships between architects and tenants or potential tenants should be in future.

• There is a lot to be said for the view that the notion of what is at present called community architecture deserves to be applied more widely than it usually is at present, more widely in two senses. The community technical aid lobby is right to point to the need to involve other professions as well as architects, and for residents to be consulted in what might be called community – or neighbourhood – planning as well as in the design of blocks of flats and low-rise housing estates.

• The case for more, and more systematic, evaluation is as strong with community architecture (and any extensions of it) as with the other examples in this report.

References

1. N. Wates and C. Knevitt, *Community Architecture: How People Are Creating Their Own Environment*, Harmondsworth, Penguin, 1987, p.29.
2. L. Kuper, 'Blueprint for living together', in L. Kuper (editor), *Living in Towns*, London, Cresset Press, 1953.
3. The pioneer of this kind of study, including physical surveys of the use of dwellings by tenants as well as interviews with them, was Oliver Cox, first when a senior architect at the London County

Council, then as Chief Architect at the then Ministry of Housing and Local Government. See, for example, Ministry of Housing and Local Government, *Family Houses at West Ham: an Account of the Project With an Appraisal*, Design Bulletin 15, London, HMSO, 1969; Ministry of Housing and Local Government, *Families Living at High Density: a Study of Estates in Leeds, Liverpool and London*, Design Bulletin 21, London, HMSO, 1970.

4. Wates and Knevitt, op.cit., p.77.
5. Royal Institute of British Architects (RIBA), *Community Projects Fund: Report*, London, RIBA, duplicated, 1986, p.4; Royal Institute of British Architects Community Architects Group, *Practising Community Architecture*, London, undated.
6. Wates and Knevitt, op.cit., p.26.
7. J. Thompson, *Community Architecture: the Story of Lea View House*, Hackney, London, Royal Institute of British Architects, 1984.
8. Wates and Knevitt, op.cit., p.74.
9. T. Woolley, *Community Architecture: the Case for User Participation in Architectural Design*, Oxford Polytechnic PhD Thesis, 1985
10. S. Tribe, 'Community casebook', *Building Design*, 21 November 1986, p.9.

10 Eight Briefer Portraits

This chapter looks, more briefly than in the previous chapters, at eight further selected examples of community-based initiatives: community work, community organisations, community development, community arts, community media, community social work, community education and community businesses.

With each of these in turn three questions are asked: what has the particular activity to do with community, what is its geographical scale, and what judgement can be made about its impact?

Community work
Community work represents a deliberate attempt, developed over the last quarter of a century, to apply professional skills to the promotion of community action and community sense. There were only a handful of community workers in the early 1950s. In 1983 over 5,300 paid staff in the United Kingdom were mainly employed on community work. Over half of them worked for voluntary organisations, and most of the rest for local authorities, in education, social services or other departments[1].

Everybody recognises that a range of other people do some of the same things. These include some of the 5,000 or so youth officers and youth workers, some of the staff of Community Relations Councils, Councils of Voluntary Service and Rural Community Councils, welfare rights workers, people working with self-help groups and of course countless clergymen, social workers and unpaid volunteers including residents themselves. The following discussion, drawing on David Thomas's analysis of community work[2], concentrates on it as a profession, although obviously much of what is said also applies to some extent to similar work done by others.

The distinctive method of work is to help people join together in meeting a need or resolving a problem that they themselves identify. Community workers provide encouragement, advice and support to groups and projects of the kinds discussed in Chapter 5. They often play a key role in launching and running community projects, in setting up new community groups and in supporting existing ones.

Their work has two different sets of aims. The first is to help people meet an identified need or problem. This has been described as a material or distributive aim, the objective being to acquire or redirect a flow of goods, services or benefits to improve the circumstances of the community in question.

The second set of aims is described as developmental. It is concerned less with immediate gains than with helping people to develop their aptitudes and capacities, both individually and collectively. The objective is to enable people to 'grow' and at the same time to work more effectively in groups, thus developing what Thomas in his book calls 'community coherence' but in the terminology of the present report would be called community attachment. The three main aims under this developmental heading are

- To help men and women acquire skills, knowledge and confidence.
- To promote political awareness and knowledge. The suggestion here is that, through participation in groups dealing with immediate needs or problems, people develop greater political maturity, thus in the long run strengthening representative democracy.
- To help the creation and development of local formal organisations and informal and semi-formal groups, thus strengthening community attachment in the locality.

One of the arguments advanced in favour of community work is about its role in inner city and other deprived areas. Community workers are currently concentrated in such places, just as 20 years ago they mainly worked in what were at the time seen as the most socially undeveloped areas – new towns and new housing estates. The inner areas are, rightly, judged to be among the places where social skills and resources are now at their weakest. Community workers are experienced in working with those most affected by poverty, inadequate housing and education, and with those who for reasons of class, income, race or sex are less likely than others to be, or to feel, involved and significant in local community life.

Community workers usually operate at a fairly local level, the scale commonly being a housing estate or an area smaller than a ward but ranging from a single street to a borough or a town. They often work with particular groups, interest communities such as young unemployed black people or the parents of under-fives, rather than with the general population.

A national structure for community work was considered by a working party under the auspices of the Gulbenkian Foundation, and its report published[3]. Attempts have been made, through the Standing Conference for Community Development, to implement the Gulbenkian proposal for a national body. Agreement has been reached by the various participants about the form of the proposed national structure, but plans are held up because of the lack of adequate resources to launch it.

Community organisations

In principle the term community organisation could properly be applied to any organised body or group which seeks to operate on behalf of a community, but it is used more narrowly by the National Federation of Community Organisations (NFCO) to refer to its actual or potential constituents, which are local federal or umbrella organisations 'concerned...with the general well-being of their neighbourhoods or communities'. For the NFCO the community is usually a locality, the geographical area being a good deal smaller than that of a district or borough council, and often described as a neighbourhood. In recent years the NFCO has also recognised the importance of communities of interest, such as an Asian or Afro-Caribbean community in a town, whose needs can also be legitimately served by an umbrella community organisation covering a wider geographical area.

The NFCO was formerly the National Federation of Community Associations (NFCA) and its present activities and interests reflect this ancestry. Developing out of the inter-war concern on the part of the then National Council of Social Service with the social problems of new housing estates and the 'depressed areas', the NFCA was founded in 1945, on the wave of enthusiasm for community centres and community associations.

In the immediate post-war period 'the community association idea reached a pinnacle of popularity which it has never quite regained', to quote the report of a working party set up in 1978 to consider the NFCA's future[4]. The Federation realised that, while the original conception had lost some of its appeal, new kinds of community group, neighbourhood group and tenants' group had flourished. The working party proposed, and the Federation accepted, a number of modifications: the Federation changed its name, it sought to develop links with related national bodies, and it broadened its membership to include new types of group (a change reflected in an increase of nearly a third in the number of affiliated bodies).

The NFCO supports its 1,200 constituent bodies in a variety of ways. These include promoting new community organisations; providing information, advice and practical help to existing community organisations; encouraging new ideas and promoting sound management; bringing people together for mutual support and to share experience; and giving voice to common interest and concerns. To be full members of NFCO local organisations have to be 'open to people of all religious and political persuasions'. They are seen by NFCO as 'democratic societies writ small'; as with community work, one of the aims is to encourage 'education for democracy' and thus 'contribute more effectively in the wider democracy'. An underlying belief is that 'identification with the neighbourhood' is 'extremely valuable both for people, as human beings, and for the health of a democratic society'.

More immediate purposes of the local umbrella organisations include the following.

- Offering other local organisations accommodation for meetings and other activities.
- Offering other organisations and local residents facilities such as duplicating, and also access to advice and information.
- Co-ordinating and organising joint activities.
- Providing direct services such as creches, adult education classes and clubs.
- Acting as a link and a representative body in dealing with the local authority or other public bodies.
- Providing a forum to decide upon a response to proposals from, for example, the local council or health authority, or to develop new schemes, for example to help disabled or elderly people.

The NFCO believes that its constituent bodies could, with support, do more along these lines, and could play a central part in any general proposals to extend community involvement and participation. Little assessment has, however, been undertaken of the contribution made by NFCO or local community organisations.

Community development

Community development is related to both community work and community organisations. But the concept, like that of community itself, is sometimes used so generally as to be difficult to pin down – it is broad in scope and ambitious in aims.

For example the working party set up by the Gulbenkian Foundation to consider a national structure for community work described community development as bringing together a number of different elements in a 'strategy for achieving the involvement of people, through their organisations, groups and institutions, in the formulation, implementation, maintenance and revision of social policy at both local and central government level'[5]. The working party added that local people 'should not only participate in shaping and operating policies but that they have a necessary, indeed a central, place in these processes, since it is the wellbeing and development of these very people which is the objective of social policies'.

A study by Maurice Broady and Rodney Hedley of community development by local authorities in England and Wales also tried to define the term[6]. (Incidentally, they found from their survey that about a third of councils had 'an active concern for community development' and that of these about a third were 'extensively involved'.) Broady and Hedley began by defining community development fairly narrowly. In the questionnaire they sent to local councils they said that they were interested in 'the way in which your local authority deliberately stimulates and encourages people to express their needs; supports them in their collective action; and helps them with their projects and schemes'. But, as they point out, many authorities explained that they used the term more broadly – to refer to 'any effort on their part to relate their services more responsively'.

Broady and Hedley distinguished six categories along a continuum from the most top-down (the provision of community facilities) to the most bottom-up (community self-government):

- community provision by the local authority;

- community consultation through public meetings or consultative bodies;
- community co-option, where local people, usually through voluntary organisations, are encouraged to carry out particular activities or take responsibility for particular services;
- community management, where local people take on responsibility for running for example a community centre provided by the council;
- community action to express local people's views, as for example through a tenants' association or a protest campaign;
- community control, 'in which the local group has a responsibility for fund-raising and an ability to take action in its own right as a fully autonomous body'; a neighbourhood council is an example.

The authors also went on to identify a number of different ways in which local authorities themselves interpreted community development in practice: as liaison with parish councils; as providing community facilities; as decentralising services; as the self-management of buildings; as consultation and participation in service delivery; as coopting voluntary organisations; as local welfare planning; as general support for the voluntary sector; as extending democracy.

These sets of headings are useful as indications of the breadth of meaning that can be given to the term, and they show something – but by no means all – of the range of applications. As explained, the specific study was in a local authority context and community development can, of course, be the aim and the approach in indigenous activities and in many top-down contexts other than local government. As well as applying to much of what is done by community workers and by community organisations, it can be seen as part of what is done by community groups and projects, and in, for example, community policing and community architecture as well as local government decentralisation.

Community arts

Some community arts projects are conceived and developed in association with community organisations or with the help of community workers. Indeed, some community workers are specialist community arts workers. Some years ago the Gulbenkian Foundation joined the Arts Council in sponsoring a study and a conference on the relationship between community work and community arts[7].

The distinctive features and aims of community arts seem to be as follows.

- Community arts are innovative and cover a range far wider than conventional arts (examples include film making, crafts, photography, inflatables, jazz and firework displays).
- They are intended to be less remote than conventional arts from people's daily lives, closer to their own concerns and interests.
- In particular, they are intended to be relevant to the life of the community: 'One of the aims...is to stimulate people to an active concern for the needs and aspirations of the community of which they form part'[8].
- They are intended to reach a wider public than the overwhelmingly middle-class audience for traditional or conventional arts.
- They are intended to be participative, done by people themselves with the support and help of community artists: 'not art for the masses but masses of art created by masses of people'[9].
- They are intended to help people realise their potential individually and to develop community sense.

Most community arts projects are local, serving the population of a particular geographical area, usually between that of a neighbourhood and of a lower-tier local authority. The products are open to all residents, as for example with a community festival, a community arts centre, a community cinema, or a community theatre – a term which may mean that it uses non-professional actors or that its productions are intended to connect with people's lives and interests in ways in which those of the conventional theatre (whether commercial or subsidised) do not.

Some events or facilities are, however, often intended not for the general local population but for particular groups locally such as children, unemployed people, elderly people or ethnic groups. Some projects are not locally based. These include touring companies and schemes to promote, for example, puppetry or the arts and culture of a particular ethnic group.

Community arts groups and projects have been funded by the Arts Council of Great Britain. After 1979 the Council devolved most of its responsibility for funding community arts to the 12 Regional Arts associations in England. The amount spent is relatively small – about 2 per cent of the Arts Council's total budget – and has not increased to any extent in recent years. Apart from local arts centres and community festivals, most of this money goes to projects in drama, music, dance, photography and murals. Community arts projects are also funded by a range of other official bodies, including local authorities and the government's Urban Programme, and by commercial sponsors.

In 1976 the Arts Council set up a Community Arts Evaluation Working Group to assess the contribution of community arts. The council had supported community arts projects for an experimental period and it sought guidance about future policy. In particular it asked the working group:

> To assess whether the extra subsidy during the two-year experiment has had a significant effect on local communities, resulting in greater creative activity.

The working group, reporting in 1977, concluded that, although adequate evidence for judgement was not by then available from a third of the projects funded, the extra subsidy had had 'a significant effect on at least half the communities involved, resulting in greater creative activity', and that it 'felt confident' of success in another quarter[10]. Thus the group's general judgement was favourable, although it must be said that the evaluation was not a very rigorous one.

A more recent study in Greater London set out to examine the audience for community arts in three areas with community arts projects[11]. The research included 'focussed population surveys'; the samples contained larger than average proportions of women, black people and unemployed people respectively in the three areas, because these had been particular targets for projects supported by the Greater London Council. The research also included sample surveys of users of the projects. The researchers found that relatively large proportions of people knew about the projects, that as many as two-fifths had actually been to one of them and that women, black people and unemployed people were well-represented among users.

The users' surveys also showed, however, that more educated people (those with O levels or higher qualifications) used the projects much more fully than less educated people, and furthermore that a majority were Labour voters. Thus, although the projects were succeeding in reaching some of the wider audience they sought, they were disproportionately attracting particular kinds of people – more educated people and Labour voters – rather than the general population of their areas. There is no way of knowing whether these findings would apply elsewhere.

Community media
In 1985 the then Home Secretary announced that he was proposing to invite bids for 21 community radio stations, to be run for a two-year experimental period from 1986. In 1986 his successor explained that futher investigation had uncovered 'various difficulties...and anxieties' and that the future of community radio would be considered as part of a wider review. The promised Green Paper on radio was published in 1987, and a White Paper on broadcasting (containing a short section on radio) in 1988[12].

The White Paper said that the government's proposals for radio, looking to advertising and sponsorship rather than public funding for all independent stations, would 'create an environment in which community radio, based on a combination of local identity and cultural diversity, will be able to fulfil its potential'. In March 1989 the government endorsed a proposal by the Independent Broadcasting Authority to seek tenders for an initial 20 community radio stations.

The Community Radio Association (CRA) defines community radio as:

> ...a system of locally-owned, democratically-controlled open access radio. A community radio station comes into existence, and develops, in response to the perceived need of a community, and is supported and run by the community which it serves[13].

It is generally recognised that the communities served may be either territorial or interest communities. The government, in its 1985 proposals, envisaged two distinct forms of community radio: the 'neighbourhood' concept, with a service radius of five kilometres, and the 'communities of interest' concept, with a larger service radius 'broadcasting to, for example, an ethnic group or those interested in a particular type of music'.

The geographical scale, even of 'neighbourhood' community radio, is larger than with most other community initiatives. The population reached by a 'neighbourhood' station in an urban area with a service radius of five kilometres would be about 300,000. The potential population for an 'interest community' station would be over a million.

There are some potential problems of ownership and accountability, although the enthusiasts make light of them. It is easy to say, as the CRA does, that community radio stations would 'have ownership solely representative of their locality or community of interest', but it would in practice be difficult to ensure such representativeness.

The supporters make large claims for community radio: it would extend free speech, give a voice to groups 'currently under-represented in existing media', stimulate local economic activity and reduce unemployment, generate more respect for diverse cultures, and 'stimulate community life, activity and well-being' (CRA). Another enthusiast has said that community radio stations 'might well have a role to play in helping to alleviate the present demoralisation and evident breakdown in communications in some of our inner cities'[14].

To sum up, the main hoped-for benefits from community radio are
• Information and advice would be given at a more local level than at present.
• Interest would be stimulated in local issues, thus promoting political education.
• Non-professionals would play a large part, helped by sympathetic professionals.
• The participating non-professionals would develop confidence and new skills.

One of the main arguments for community radio seems, however, to be more concerned with developing alternatives to the commercial or state ways of doing things than with these or any of the other standard 'community' objectives:

> It is, in fact, the alternative nature of community media which best explains their character, rather than the word 'community', whose vagueness causes problems. The approach involves putting the local community (or its constituent 'communities of interest') first, rather than the dictates of admass, scheduling or artistic or professional excellence[15].

Community newspapers, printers, publishers and bookshops mainly serve relatively small-scale geographical areas (smaller than a local authority district or borough); with the help of new technologies they have developed substantially in recent years. They have some of the same aims as other community projects – opportunities for people to develop skills, relevance to community interests, encouragement of political awareness and of community sense – and they share with other community media the desire to offer an alternative channel of communication, not dominated by professionals, and neither profit-dominated nor paternalistic.

Community social work
Community social work is closely linked with two other community policies examined in previous chapters: it is often one element in local government decentralisation (Chapter 6) and it also operates within the broader framework of community care (Chapter 7).

The idea of community social work was first raised in the Seebohm Report on the personal social services in 1968[16], and was developed in the Barclay Report on social workers in 1982[17]. Barclay emphasised the importance of 'tapping' and 'underpinning' the informal networks that provide the bulk of social care (that is, non-financial and non-medical care. The report said:

> The large majority of people in the categories served by the personal social services who are unable to care for themselves, receive their principal support from relatives. Friends and neighbours also often play a significant role.

The contribution of other networks, including self-help groups, was also acknowledged in the report. The report recognised that 'caring networks' can be local or non-local.

The importance of such support systems led the working party to argue that it was 'essential for the personal social services providing social care on a formal basis to work in close understanding with informal caring networks and not in isolation from them'. The essence of the proposal was a new partnership between the two sides, to include 'conferring some share in decision-making on local communities and mutual help and self-help groups'.

Partly because informal caring arrangements vary greatly from area to area, and partly also because the Report recognised that informal networks are not necessarily local, it left open the question of detailed organisation, suggesting 'not a blue print but the development of flexible decentralised patterns of organisation'. In discussing examples, it pointed to two main approaches adopted so far. One focusses on locality, social workers being organised into 'patch' teams covering small local areas. This option was strongly favoured by the authors of a minority appendix to the Report, who called it 'neighbourhood-based' social work. The other approach was concerned instead with particular client groups, for example elderly people and families with children, each such group being served by a specialist team.

Patch area teams usually cover populations of 20,000 to 30,000, with sub-teams covering 10,000. Specialist teams cover much larger parts of a local authority area, sometimes all of it.

A number of doubts have been raised about the proposals; in particular, Robert Pinker, a member of the Barclay Committee, wrote a minority appendix. His first worry was about accountability. He feared that sharing 'decision-making' with client groups and informal networks would make for conflict and confusion, increase costs and delay service delivery. Presumably the majority of the working party recognised the problem, but believed that power-sharing between the formal and informal sectors was essential and that in any case the ultimate responsibility for formal social work clearly rested with elected representatives.

Pinker's second concern was about privacy: he argued that, in seeking out potential informal support and trying to develop it, social workers might sometimes try to impose informal networks on people who did not want them. A related criticism was that neighbours, for instance, might not wish to become involved with certain kinds of social work client. The same worry had been expressed by Philip Abrams earlier[18]. More generally, it has been suggested that Barclay exaggerates the extent to which untapped sources of informal care exist[19].

Again those favouring community social work acknowledge these worries, but argue that the basic line remains sound. They would suggest that we know enough already to give guidance about which kinds of people are likely to worry about privacy and on whose behalf particular delicacy needs to be exercised, and which are likely to be relatively unconcerned.

Since Barclay, further research has been carried out on patch and on an alternative approach laying emphasis on decentralising resources to help the people in most acute need decentralisating services[20], but the debate continues, and doubts remain about the best method of implementing community social work[21]. There is, however, agreement about the general objective of linking social work more effectively with the informal care and support given by relatives and others.

Community education

Henry Morris, who was Director of Education for Cambridgeshire in the inter-war years, is usually credited with launching the concept of community education. Morris, believing that educational institutions could play an important part in bringing residents together and enriching their collective lives, founded Cambridgeshire's 'village colleges', based on secondary schools and with a range of additional educational and cultural functions. The Cambridge example was emulated in Britain and abroad, and taken up in urban areas as well as rural.

In the post-war period, a number of official reports such as the 1959 Albermarle Report[22] gave new impetus to using schools (sometimes through the addition of special wings) for adult education, the youth service, sports and recreation. These developments were mainly associated with secondary schools.

The Plowden Report of 1967 gave a different emphasis. Plowden was concerned with primary education, and laid strong emphasis on the influence of parental aspirations and concern upon the performance of children at that stage. More 'open' primary schools were seen as means of stimulating parental interest and thus, in particular, helping disadvantaged children in educationally deprived areas: 'Community schools...would be open beyond ordinary school hours for the use of children, their parents and, exceptionally, for other members of the community'[23]. This limited concept of community schools in the primary sector – with access confined mainly to parents – was subsequently broadened by enthusiasts (particularly some of those associated with the Educational Priority Area experiments), who envisaged a wider role for primary schools in serving and linking with their communities.

In the 1970s there was increasing enthusiasm for developing community education in adult education. One aim was to reach out 'to new sectors of the population and to discover needs which adult education can be instrumental in meeting in, for example, an immigrant community, an area of urban redevelopment, a day centre for the mentally handicapped or a home for the elderly'[24]. Some of those concerned with adult education are concerned that this emphasis 'on social therapy and community development' may be at the cost of serious education for adults.

Whether in community schools or in adult education, community education has been taken up by many local authorities: 'well over half of the local authorities have invested resources to varying degrees in one form of community education or another since the Second World War'[25]. This development has been possible partly because community education has seldom been seen as a political issue. It has also been helped by the encouragement of the Department of Education and Science, and particularly its Architects and Building Group. Sometimes new community schools (usually comprehensive secondary schools) have been located in purpose-built 'centres' or 'complexes', including such joint facilities as a theatre, sports centre, swimming pool, library or restaurant. There have also been schemes for community sharing of the facilities of primary schools and of further education colleges and polytechnics[26].

Schools often have catchment areas or at least serve notional local populations. Thus the population of a local community sharing primary school facilities would in principle be about 5,000 and that sharing a secondary school between about 10,000 and 20,000. It may be noted that one argument put by the Plowden Report was that, because primary schools have a small catchment area, 'they are more genuinely neighbourhood schools' – in other words are more local – than other schools or colleges.

The population figures cited apply to community schools operating on limited Plowden assumptions, that is where the main emphasis is on linking the school with the parents of its pupils. But with schools containing community facilities the population drawn upon is larger. The shared facilites, from meeting rooms and snack bars (primary schools) to theatres and swimming pools (secondary schools) are not provided at all the schools in an area but only at some. Furthermore, the people who become associated with the school are, particularly among those living outside the immediate vicinity, likely to be a self-selected minority. The catchment area for all adult community education is likely to be larger than for schools, because the numbers taking part are again a relatively small proportion of the population. With community polytechnics and further education colleges the participating proportion is even smaller, the territorial community drawn upon even more dispersed geographically and participation even more of a minority and self-selective kind, a point made explicitly in the Progress Report by the Department of Education and Science on the Abraham Moss Centre, an 'educational and community project' in Manchester:

> The implication...is that the community is the people living in the area and that Abraham Moss should become their centre. The reality is...otherwise[27].

From Henry Morris onwards, community education has been seen as much more than the use by residents of the space and facilities of schools or colleges. John Nisbet and his colleagues, in an evaluation of community education in the Grampian region of Scotland, distinguish some of the broader objectives. Drawing upon their discussion, the following aims can be identified.

- The development of a 'community-oriented curriculum' in schools and colleges.
- The encouragement of 'life-long education'.
- Community involvement in decision making and management.
- Mutually supportive relationships between school and community.
- The development of social groupings and of a sense of attachment with the local community[28].

The Nisbet research is particularly valuable because systematic evaluation is so rare. Their book is the report of a three-year investigation, covering both primary and secondary schools and comprising general surveys and five case studies. Though the research was in Scotland, whose educational system is different from that in England and Wales, it seems reasonable to assume that in general terms the findings would apply elsewhere. The authors conclude that there are clear advantages in integrating community facilities with school buildings, and they draw some lessons about organisation and management. As to the more ambitious aims, they say that, though the changes observed were 'incremental' rather than 'radical', some progress was being made. They summed up:

> We should therefore take care not to expect too much too soon of the community school movement, nor make the opposite mistake of underrating its educational significance because of its apparently slow rate of growth.

Community business

With community business the concern is with people's role as producers as well as consumers. The central aim is to establish, in areas of high unemployment, local schemes providing paid jobs additional to those generated in the standard labour market by commercial and public employers. As well as creating jobs, community businesses produce useful goods or services which can improve the locality or the lives of its disadvantaged residents.

Such schemes are sometimes described as community enterprises. There is a danger of semantic confusion over both terms. First, community businesses have nothing directly to do with the similar sounding Business in the Community (BiC), an association of firms and other employers established to encourage industrial and commercial firms to play a part in their local community (see Appendix). Although local enterprise agencies are set up by BiC seek to help small businesses, these are normally seen as ordinary commercial firms. Secondly, the term community enterprise is sometimes used differently, as with the Community Enterprise Scheme organised by *The Times* and the Royal Institute of British Architects with the Prince of Wales as Patron. This is an annual competition, which is open to community-initiated building projects.

Community businesses developed first in Scotland, starting from the late 1970s. More has been written about the Scottish experience, and a definition suggested by Community Business Scotland is often cited:

> ...a trading organisation which is owned and controlled by the local community and which aims to create self-supporting and viable jobs for local people in its area of benefit, and to use any profits made from its business activities to create more employment, to provide local services or to support local charitable work[29].

A recent review of community business, carried out for the Department of the Environment by Land and Urban Analysis Limited (LAURA), gave a fuller list of objectives:

* *Ownership and control by the community which the business serves.* The authors point out that, although the community in question is usually a local territorial community, it is sometimes a wider community of interest, for example members of a particular ethnic community in a town.

- *To be a good employer*, 'that is, to pay fair and reasonable wages, to operate an equal opportunities policy...to be concerned for the individual's development and career prospects and, where possible, offer training in transferable skills'.
- *To be democratically managed*, both internally and in the relationship between the management board and the community served.
- *Creation of work for the long-term unemployed and for disadvantaged groups in the labour market.*
- *To be a focus for local economic and community development* 'by developing a range of trading activities and empowering the community to start and run small enterprises...'.
- *To channel profits into purposes of community benefit and into economic regeneration activities.*
- *To provide goods and services which the community needs* 'at prices which are within its means'[30].

The 14 case studies in the LAURA review illustrate the range. One of the community businesses studied ran a public park, including an experimental farm. Two others were garden centres, selling plants and garden accessories and providing advice on urban gardens. A fourth focussed on music; it ran concerts and discos, rented out cheap rehearsal facilities and advised budding musicians. Another recycled furniture, offering it at discounted prices to needy clients. Some were in effect clusters of projects or were holding companies running or helping several enterprises. One rented out small industrial units, while its sister projects carried out building maintenance, made joinery products and offered enterprise training and advice.

Support for community business projects comes from a range of sources, including local authorities, the European Community, the Urban Programme and (in the past) the Manpower Services Commission's Community Programme. Examples of projects which have received funding from other government agencies as well as the MSC, are community insulation schemes and community refurbishment schemes. Both provide jobs for people who have been out of work for a long time, the first employing them to put heating insulation into the homes of people receiving income support, the second to refurbish run-down council estates.

As the LAURA report pointed out, there can be tensions between the different objectives of particular community businesses. Schemes vary in the extent to which residents or other interests in the community own or control projects. They vary in how far their emphasis is on production or on consumption – in creating jobs as against producing a benefit to the community in the form of goods or services. Community businesses vary too in whether they can, after an initial two to five years, become self-sufficient or whether, because of management difficulties or because the goods or services produced are not commercially marketable, they can survive only with continuing subsidies.

A study of community businesses in Clydeside offered a limited list of criteria – the personal development of participants, the 'community effect, material and psychological', temporary and permanent jobs created – and referred to these in making its assessment:

> The first two elements are difficult to measure... If we focus on employment...then the effect is so far limited... Community businesses have provided a number of temporary jobs and some more permanent self-supporting employment[31].

They added that there were 'indirect social savings through reducing tensions generated by unemployment, including crime, vandalism and ill-health, and the provision of necessary services which otherwise do not exist', but said that they were not able to measure these.

Another study, of Scottish experience more widely, concluded:

> ...at present, community business remains far removed from the ideals... Some new economic activity has been stimulated in deprived areas and jobs and incomes have been provided for marginal workers in the labour market. But this constitutes only a small dent in the problem and most community businesses remain fragile concerns, dependent on outside support and subsidy[32].

The LAURA researchers commented that 'the community business movement...is new and is finding its way' and that the schemes 'face formidable difficulties'. The LAURA review went further than other studies, in trying to define and promote good practice, rather than assessing the success or failure of community business. Under a range of headings such as 'project planning', 'sources of capital', 'financial planning and control', 'marketing and promotion', 'premises and location', it listed scores of 'points of good practice'. These constitute a battery of useful practical advice to community businesses themselves and to agencies which fund and support them. For example, community businesses are advised to do 'thorough market research' and to define their objectives clearly. They should 'chase unpaid invoices', make careful cash-flow projections, monitor them monthly, and carry out regular cost analysis. Funding and support agencies are advised, for instance, that 'financial support needs to be provided for a community development function', that 'loans, rather than grants, make a budget go further', and that 'community businesses need advice on how to estimate training costs, how to obtain grants to cover them, and where to find the kind of training courses which will meet their individual requirements'.

This LAURA study shows the value of an analyses designed to provide the basis for practical guidance. Not only community businesses, but other community initiatives as well, would benefit both from more attempts at objective assessment of experience and from similar guides to good practice.

*   *   *   *   *

The previous five chapters examined particular community initiatives at some length. This chapter has looked at eight further examples, and others are listed in the Appendix. The broader discussion in Part I draws upon all these sources.

References

1. D. Francis, P. Henderson and D.N. Thomas, *A Survey of Community Workers in the United Kingdom*, London, National Institute for Social Work, 1984.
2. D.N. Thomas, *The Making of Community Work*, London, George Allen and Unwin, 1983.
3. Calouste Gulbenkian Foundation, *A National Centre for Community Development*, The Report of a Working Party, London, Calouste Gulbenkian Foundation, 1984.
4. National Federation of Community Associations, *Tomorrow's Community*, London, Bedford Square Press, 1979.

5. Calouste Gulbenkian Foundation, *A National Centre for Community Development*, Report of a Working Party, London, 1984, paragraph 18.
6. M. Broady and R. Hedley, *Working Partnerships: Community Development in Local Authorities*, London, Bedford Square Press for the National Coalition of Neighbourhoods, 1989.
7. Arts Council/Calouste Gulbenkian Foundation, *The Relationship of Community Arts to Community Work*, London, Arts Council of Great Britain/Calouste Gulbenkian Foundation, 1979.
8. Arts Council of Great Britain, *Community Arts: A Report by the Arts Council's Community Arts Evaluation Working Group*, London, Arts Council of Great Britain, 1977.
9. Arts Council of Great Britain, *Community Arts: the Report of the Community Arts Working Party*, London, Arts Council of Great Britain, 1974.
10. Arts Council of Great Britain, 1977, op.cit.
11. J. Lewis, D. Morley and R. Southwood, *Art: Who Needs It? The Audience for Community Arts*, London, Comedia, 1986.
12. Home Office, *Radio: Choice and Opportunities*, a Consultative Document, Cm 92, London, HMSO, 1987; Home Office, *Broadcasting in the '90s; Competition, Choice and Quality*, Cm 517, London, HMSO, 1988.
13. Community Radio Association (CRA), *Community Radio: an Open door to Media Access*, Bristol, Community Radio Association, 1986.
14. S. Partridge, 'Community radio: an idea whose time has come?' *Voluntary Action*, Autumn 1981.
15. P. Lewis, *Community Television and Cable in Britain*, London, British Film Institute, 1978.
16. Seebohm Report, *Report of the Committee on Local Authority and Allied Social Services*, Cmnd 3703, London, HMSO, 1968.
17. Barclay Report, *Social Workers: their Role and Tasks*, London, Bedford Square Press for National Institute for Social Work, 1982.
18. P. Abrams, 'Social change, social networks and neighbourhood care', *Social Work Service*, 22, 1980.
19. G. Allan, 'Informal networks of care: issues raised by Barclay', *British Journal of Social Work*, 13(4)23, 1983; M. Bulmer, *The Social Basis of Community Care*, London, George Allen and Unwin, 1987.

20. On patch experiments see R. Hadley and M. McGrath (editors), *Going Local: Neighbourhood Social Services*, London, Bedford Square Press, 1981 and R. Hadley and M. McGrath, *When Social Services Are Local*, London, George Allen and Unwin, 1984. On the alternative 'Kent Community Care' experiment see B. Davies and D. Challis, *Matching Resources to Needs in Community Care*, Aldershot, Gower for Personal Social Services Research Unit, 1986 and D. Challis and B. Davies, *Case Management in Community Care*, Aldershot, Gower for Personal Social Services Research Unit, 1986.

21. P. Willmott, *Social Networks, Informal Care and Public Policy*, London, Policy Studies Institute, 1986, pp.111-115.

22. Albemarle Report, *Report of the Committee on the Youth Service in England and Wales*, Cmnd 929, London, HMSO, 1960.

23. Plowden Report, *Children and their Primary Schools*, A Report of the Central Advisory Council for Education, England, 2 vols, London, HMSO, 1967.

24. G. Mee and H. Wiltshire, *Structure and Performance in Adult Education*, London, Longman, 1978, p.82.

25. B. O'Hagan, 'Community education in Britain', in G. Allen, J. Bastiani, I. Martin and K. Richards (editors), *Community Education: an Agenda for Educational Reform*, Milton Keynes, Open University, 1987, p.73)

26. G. Kenny, *Polytechnics: the Shared Use of Space and Facilities*, London, Department of Education and Science, 1977; Department of Education and Science, *Victoria Centre, Crewe: School and Community Provision in Urban Renewal*, Building Bulletin 59, London, HMSO, 1981; Department of Education and Science Architects and Building Group, *Community Use of Primary Schools*, Broadsheet 15, London, Department of Education and Science, 1983.

27. Department of Education and Science Architects and Building Branch, *Abraham Moss Centre, Manchester: Project Report, A and B*, Paper 1/78, London, Department of Education and Science, 1978.

28. J. Nisbet, L. Hendry, C. Stewart and J. Watt, *Towards Community Education*, Aberdeen, Aberdeen University Press, 1980.

29. Proposal for an experimental funding programme for community businesses in Scotland submitted to the European Community by Community Business Scotland, September 1981.
30. Land and Urban Analysis Limited (LAURA), *Community Business: Best Practice in Urban Regeneration*, Vol. I, pp. 21-22.
31. C. Moore and V. Skinner, *Community Business in the Clydeside Conurbation*, The Inner City in Context Working Paper 2, Department of Social and Economic Research, University of Glasgow, undated.
32. A. McArthur, 'An unconventional approach to economic development: the role of community business', *Town Planning Review*, 57 (1), 1986, pp.87-100.

Appendix
Further Community Initiatives

Further community concepts and initiatives noted in the course of the review.

Business in the Community (BiC) – 'an association of major UK businesses committed to working in partnership with each other, with central and local government, voluntary organisations and trade unions to promote social responsibility and revitalise economic life in local communities'. (See for example *Business in the Community Review of the Year 1988*, BiC, 227A City Road, London, EC1V 1LX)

Community accounting – helps community groups to handle their accounts, for example in Nottingham the Community Accountancy Support Service 'provides an administrative and bookkeeping rescue service, free auditing and training and advice sessions to voluntary organisations and small businesses'. (*Voluntary Action, New Society*, 24 January 1986)

Community Action Trust – set up in Autumn 1987, as the sponsor for Crime Stoppers in Britain (Crime Stopper organisations exist in the United States); the Trust will 'fund rewards to people who help police with information about crimes of violence...the scheme has been welcomed by Scotland Yard'. (*Guardian*, 24 June 1987)

Community Aide Programme – 'matches physically and mentally handicapped people in a partnership which is planned to yield equal benefit to both groups'. (A. Whitehouse, *Community Care*, 8 March 1984)

Community bus – see 'community transport'.

Community computing – provides training and access to computers to disadvantaged people in order to improve their prospects; helps community groups to use computers in their administration; aims at 'exposing and demystifying unfair uses of computers in employment or as an instrument of state control'. (P. Rowan of Community Computing Network, quoted in K. Edwards, *Voluntary Action, New Society*, 9 January 1987)

Community Councils (Scotland) – established under the Local Government (Scotland) Act 1973 to '...ascertain, co-ordinate and express to the local authorities for its area, and to public authorities, the views of the community which it represents, in relation to matters for which those authorities are responsible, and to take such action in the interests of that community as appears to it to be expedient and practicable'. The councils are optional and have no statutory functions.

Community Councils (Wales) – under the Local Government Act 1972 what were formerly rural parishes were established as community councils, and such councils were also set up in ex-urban areas whose urban councils requested this. In functions Welsh community councils are broadly similar to parish councils in England.

Community Health Councils – created in England and Wales under the National Health Service Reorganisation Act 1973. There are similar bodies, differently named, for Scotland and Northern Ireland. Normally having the same boundaries as its district health authority, each CHC has a duty 'to represent the interests in the health service of the public in its district'. CHCs have no formal powers but have the right to ask for information, to inspect NHS premises, to be consulted about plans, to make representations, and to send one (non-voting) member to meetings of the district health authority.

Community health initiatives – projects which 'exist primarily to encourage people to take a more active interest in their own health on terms acceptable and relevant to the communities involved'. The National Council for Voluntary Organisations publishes a *Directory of Community Health Initiatives.* (P. Jay, 'Health for all: a role for the community', *Journal of the Royal College of Physicians*, 17 (2), 1983)

Community information – information supplied by libraries, Citizens Advice Bureaux and others to local people or local community groups. As well as being helped with information, community groups can sometimes have access to facilities such as typing and printing for the cost of materials only. Computers are often used to 'enable the workers in an organisation to retrieve information more effectively, thus improving the service they offer to their clients; [or] to allow the public direct access to the information'. (*At the Touch* *of a Button: a Survey of Computer Based Local Community Information Services*, Community Information Project, Bethnal Green Library, Cambridge Heath Road, London E1 0HL, January 1985)

Community music – 'an attempt to extend music beyond the traditional confines of a classically taught, formalised discipline to reach everyone, regardless of their previous experience or ability'. (J. Stephenson, 'A musical keynote', *New Society*, 26 February 1988)

Community organising – borrowing from the United States the Alinsky method to 'build broadly based, multi-issue, neighbourhood organisations that have real clout'. Not to be confused with community organisations, described in Chapter 10. (J. Pitt and M. Keane, *Community Organising: You've Never Really Tried It*, Birmingham, J and P Publications, 1984

Community photography – a branch of community arts. Photography is seen as a skill that can be acquired relatively easily (with the help of a professional community photographer), and then applied by local people in their own area. Community photography is also used, by professionals or non-professionals, to document local activities or promote local campaigns. (M. Abbott, 'Community photography', *Scope*, March 1983)

Community planning councils – proposed for England and Wales by a Public Participation Working Party of the Royal Town Planning Institute (1982). The report has not been endorsed by the RTPI Council, but was circulated for discussion. The model is the Community Health Council (q.v.). CPCs would be established initially in metropolitan districts and large urban shire districts in England and Wales. Like CHCs, they would have the right of access to relevant information held by the local planning authority, and to be consulted by the authority over a range of issues.

Community Rights Project – campaigns on local government and health issues; 'concerned with the lack of community power and user rights and, in particular, the lack of information, consultation and representation' (Community Rights Project, 157 Waterloo Road, London SE1 8XF)

Community seconding – the releasing, on full- or part-time, long- or short-term, of a company employee to a community project. (Supported by Business in the Community, q.v.)

Community service orders – a new type of sentence introduced under the the Criminal Justice Act 1972, which gave the courts the power to order offenders to perform unpaid work as a service to the community. The offenders have to be 16 (formerly 17) or over. Between 40 and 240 hours have to be worked, normally within one year of the date of the order. Examples of the tasks performed are: constructing a children's playground, helping in a youth club, decorating the home of a handicapped person, clearing the garden of an elderly person, working on the renovation of a church hall.

Community transport – non-profit (often subsidised) schemes to provide transport for people who would otherwise find it difficult to get about. Many such schemes are for disabled people, who are sometimes offered individual transport (suitably converted cars, with drivers) and sometimes travel in ambulances or converted mini-buses. Other schemes provide transport at night for women. The other main category is community bus services in rural areas without public transport. The workers in community transport schemes are sometimes volunteers, sometimes paid by central or local government. (Department of Transport, *A Guide to Community Transport*, London, HMSO, 1978)

Community trusts – 'independent charitable trusts which raise funds to help meet the needs of a particular local community' (K. Edwards 'Your local trust', *Voluntary Action, New Society*, 18 December 1987, and *Community Trusts Handbook*, Community Trust Development Unit, Charities Aid Foundation, 51 St May's Road, Tonbridge, Kent TN9 2LE)